Core Mathematics Frameworks Enabling Artificial Intelligence Breakthroughs

A Clear Path Through AI Mathematical Foundations

Elliot Ramsey

Table of Contents

INTRODUCTION

The universal language of mathematics enables intelligent systems to interpret data, identify patterns, forecast outcomes, and solve increasingly complex problems. The essential power of intelligent systems lies in the mathematical principles that govern their design, learning processes, and decision-making, even though many people often associate artificial intelligence with programming, algorithms, and computer hardware. Learners who have a solid grasp of these concepts can understand not just how AI apps work but also why they behave as they do in certain situations.

For students, professionals, researchers, and inquisitive learners alike, this book presents the fundamental mathematical ideas underpinning contemporary artificial intelligence in an organized, understandable way. Instead of viewing mathematics as a collection of discrete formulas, it shows how different areas of the field collaborate to produce dependable and effective intelligent systems. With real-world applications in machine learning, data analysis, and computational problem-solving, subjects such as algebra, geometry, calculus, probability, statistics, optimization, and discrete mathematics are examined.

Readers will become more confident in their ability to comprehend complex AI concepts and critically assess upcoming technologies by building a strong mathematical foundation. The information included in these chapters helps readers make the connection between mathematical theory and practical artificial intelligence by promoting analytical reasoning, logical problem solving, and lifelong learning.

CHAPTER I
Mathematical Thinking as the Foundation of Artificial Intelligence

Understanding the Language of Mathematics in AI

Since mathematics is the foundation for intelligent systems, mastering its language is one of the most crucial elements in learning artificial intelligence. Even though programming languages, powerful computers, and sophisticated software are frequently associated with artificial intelligence, these technologies rely heavily on mathematical concepts that underpin relationships, patterns, and logical reasoning. An artificial intelligence system uses mathematical concepts rather than just intuition to govern all of its predictions, recommendations, classifications, and optimizations. Computers can express information, process data, assess uncertainty, and learn from experience thanks to mathematics' universal language. Learners gain a better understanding of how artificial intelligence works and why mathematical reasoning is crucial for creating dependable and efficient intelligent systems by mastering this mathematical language.

Concepts that might normally be challenging to convey can be precisely described thanks to mathematics. Mathematical phrases offer precise definitions and consistent norms, in contrast to everyday language, which may contain ambiguity or many interpretations. Because computers need precise instructions and quantifiable relationships, this accuracy is particularly crucial in artificial intelligence. Mathematics offers an organized framework that ensures computations remain precise and repeatable, whether calculating distances between data points, quantifying prediction errors, or enhancing learning algorithms. Mathematics is essential to the study and use of artificial intelligence because of its capacity to explain complicated concepts precisely.

Data representation is one of the main functions of mathematics in artificial intelligence. For intelligent systems to process any data, it must first be transformed into numerical form. Written language turns into numerical sequences, audio recordings into numerical waveforms, images into collections of pixel values, and customer data into structured databases. Algorithms can examine patterns that might otherwise go unnoticed thanks to these numerical representations. Meaningful learning is made possible by mathematics' ability to efficiently organize, alter, and comprehend these numerical representations.

One of the first mathematical concepts used in artificial intelligence is algebra. Equations explain the relationships between various values, whereas variables represent unknown quantities. Machine learning models use algebraic expressions to compute outputs, combine input features, and update internal parameters during training. Even relatively basic predictive models use algebraic formulas to forecast future events based on observed data. Learners can understand how artificial intelligence converts unprocessed data into practical predictions by grasping variables, equations, and functions.

Because they explain how one set of values is changed into another, functions are especially significant. Functions in artificial intelligence map inputs to outputs, enabling systems to identify connections between intended predictions and observed data. A function might, for instance, turn image attributes into object classifications or customer data into purchase suggestions. To identify extremely complicated patterns across massive datasets, more sophisticated neural networks integrate thousands or even millions of mathematical functions. Together, these features enable complex computational models to learn from their experiences.

Another crucial mathematical language for artificial intelligence is provided by linear algebra. Large sets of numerical data are organized into structured formats that computers can process effectively using vectors and matrices. A matrix retains numerous observations at once, whereas a vector may depict the features of a single observation. Because this design facilitates effective mathematical operations, matrices are often used to represent images, documents, financial information, and sensor measurements. Neural networks can handle large datasets quickly while maintaining mathematical consistency thanks to matrix multiplication, one of the most widely used operations in machine learning.

Understanding artificial intelligence is also greatly aided by geometry. Modern machine learning uses geometric principles to describe data in high-dimensional spaces, even though geometry is often associated with shapes and measurements. Every observation turns into a point in a mathematical space with several characteristics. While distinct observations occupy far-off locations, similar observations appear close to one another. To find clusters, categorize observations, and identify significant patterns, artificial intelligence programs examine these geometric correlations. Learners can better comprehend how intelligent systems differentiate between many categories and make precise predictions by seeing data geometrically.

The mathematical tools needed for learning and optimization are provided by calculus. To reduce prediction errors, machine learning models continuously adjust internal parameters during training. Gradients show paths toward increased accuracy, whereas derivatives quantify how changes in these factors affect total performance. Optimization algorithms use these mathematical ideas to continuously improve predictions. One of the most popular optimization techniques, gradient descent, shows how calculus helps AI systems learn from experience by methodically reducing errors.

Mathematical techniques for managing uncertainty are introduced by probability theory. Since real-world data is rarely comprehensive or entirely predictable, probabilistic thinking is crucial for making wise decisions. Many artificial intelligence systems assess the probability of various possibilities rather than drawing definitive conclusions. For example, instead of announcing its forecast with absolute certainty, an image recognition machine can conclude that a picture has a 95% chance of containing a bicycle. Even in situations when information is lacking, probability enables intelligent systems to assess uncertainty realistically and make well-informed decisions.

By offering techniques for evaluating data and deriving significant conclusions, statistics enhances probability. By summarizing complex datasets, statistical measures such as averages, variance, and correlations make it easier to spot significant trends. When assessing model performance, selecting relevant features, and identifying correlations in data, artificial intelligence primarily relies on statistical reasoning. Additionally, statistical inference makes it possible for machine learning models to generalize from training data to novel scenarios, guaranteeing that predictions continue to be valuable beyond previously seen examples.

Another crucial mathematical language that underpins artificial intelligence is logic. Intelligent systems can assess circumstances, adhere to regulations, and make consistent conclusions thanks to logical thinking. Logical principles are the foundation of knowledge representation frameworks, automated reasoning engines, and rule-based expert systems. Logical reasoning remains crucial for ensuring consistency, explainability, and formal correctness across a variety of applications, even though many contemporary machine learning techniques emphasize statistical learning.

To enhance model performance, optimization integrates concepts from algebra, calculus, and statistics. Artificial intelligence systems seek parameter settings that minimize unnecessary complexity and maximize forecast accuracy. Until acceptable performance is achieved, optimization algorithms continuously evaluate objective functions, compute modifications, and adjust internal parameters. During training, these mathematical processes enable models to continuously develop as they adjust to new data and shifting contexts.

Additionally, mathematics offers ways to gauge performance. To assess whether learning is progressing, artificial intelligence systems need objective standards. By contrasting model outputs with predefined target values, loss functions quantify prediction errors. Larger loss values indicate greater disparities, whereas smaller values indicate superior performance. Additional mathematical tools for evaluating model quality include accuracy, precision, recall, and other evaluation criteria. These metrics guarantee that advancements are founded on objective data rather than personal opinion.

Mathematical language encompasses abstraction and generalization in addition to specific formulas. Mathematical models frequently represent broad classes of related circumstances rather than a single problem. Because algorithms trained on representative data may apply the gained information to previously unknown samples, artificial intelligence's capacity for generalization makes it extremely versatile. By recognizing underlying structures instead of storing discrete facts, mathematical abstraction helps intelligent systems become more efficient and predictive.

Applications of artificial intelligence make the significance of mathematical language abundantly evident. To identify objects in images, computer vision systems employ geometry, linear algebra, probability, and optimization. To comprehend human speech, natural language processing integrates statistics, probability, mathematics, and optimization. To forecast preferences, recommendation systems examine mathematical correlations between users and products. While autonomous cars continuously determine the best course of action based on sensor data and geometric reasoning, medical diagnosis algorithms use statistical analysis to assess the probability of disease. Every effective application relies on mathematics supporting intelligent behavior in the background.

Analytical skills are also developed through studying the mathematical language of artificial intelligence. Learners improve their ability to reason logically, solve problems, think quantitatively, and systematically examine difficult circumstances. These abilities span a wide range of fields where data-driven decision-making is increasingly crucial, including engineering, economics, healthcare, finance, scientific research, and many more. Mathematics helps people tackle difficult problems with confidence and accuracy by encouraging deliberate, evidence-based reasoning.

To sum up, mathematics is the universal language that enables artificial intelligence. The concepts required to represent information, handle data, quantify uncertainty, assess performance, and enhance learning are provided by mathematics through algebra, functions, linear algebra, geometry, calculus, probability, statistics, logic, and optimization. These mathematical underpinnings enable intelligent systems to identify patterns, adapt to novel situations, and resolve challenging problems across a wide range of practical applications. Learners can progress from merely using artificial intelligence technologies to understanding the underlying principles by mastering the mathematical language. Mathematical expertise will remain crucial for developing creative, dependable, and accountable intelligent systems capable of handling increasingly complex problems as artificial intelligence continues to revolutionize industry and scientific research.

Building Strong Foundations in Algebra and Functions

One of the most crucial elements in understanding artificial intelligence and contemporary computer systems is developing a solid foundation in algebra and functions. Although complex algorithms, powerful computers, and enormous datasets are frequently associated with artificial intelligence, the mathematical foundations of these technologies begin with basic algebra. Algebra provides the language for identifying patterns, articulating relationships between quantities, and methodically resolving issues. Functions are crucial for depicting the behavior of intelligent systems because they expand on these concepts by specifying how one quantity depends on another. The mathematical foundation of machine learning, data analysis, optimization, and predictive modeling consists of algebra and functions. Gaining trust in these ideas helps students comprehend not just how AI systems work but also why they provide specific outcomes.

Because algebra substitutes symbols for numbers to represent unknown or variable values, it is often referred to as generalized arithmetic. Algebra is particularly useful in artificial intelligence, where data is always changing, because of its ability to handle variables. Algebra enables the development of mathematical models that apply to a wide range of scenarios, not just a single numerical problem. For instance, an algebraic equation can explain the behavior of a complete system under various conditions, as opposed to computing the result for a single input. Because of their adaptability, AI systems can handle new data without requiring entirely new instructions for every circumstance. Learners gain the capacity to articulate real-world issues in a mathematical format that computers can effectively examine by comprehending variables, expressions, and equations.

One of the most basic concepts in algebra is variables. A variable is a symbol for a quantity whose value is subject to change. Features, measurements, inputs, outputs, and model parameters are all represented as variables in artificial intelligence. Temperature, humidity, wind speed, and air pressure can all be represented by variables in a weather prediction model. A recommendation system may use variables characterizing consumer preferences, past purchases, and product attributes. Mathematical models are made simpler to comprehend, work with, and modify by assigning symbols to these quantities. Variables are essential components of intelligent algorithms because they provide the flexibility needed to model dynamic, evolving systems.

By combining variables with numbers and mathematical operations such as addition, subtraction, multiplication, and division, expressions are built. Algebraic expressions do not always provide precise values; instead, they represent relationships. They offer condensed representations of computations that would otherwise need to be explained in great detail. Expressions are frequently used in artificial intelligence to define feature transformations, scoring formulae, and algorithmic intermediate computations. To process information step-by-step, even the most sophisticated machine learning models are composed of several algebraic expressions that relate to one another. Learners can more successfully follow the computation flow of AI systems by comprehending the construction and simplification of expressions.

By representing the equality of two mathematical expressions, equations present another crucial idea. Equations are essential tools for prediction, analysis, and optimization since solving them entails determining values that fulfill these relationships. Equations are often used in artificial intelligence to represent computational models, statistical correlations, and learning objectives. Prediction models, for instance, frequently use observed data to solve equations to estimate unknown quantities. Equations specify how model parameters should be adjusted to improve accuracy in machine learning. These mathematical connections give algorithms the framework they need to convert data into insightful conclusions rather than random results.

Because AI systems frequently need to rearrange mathematical relationships to isolate unknown quantities or streamline calculations, the ability to modify equations is crucial. Researchers can create effective algorithms to handle challenging computational tasks by rearranging equations, factoring expressions, and solving systems of equations. These methods are useful tools utilized in artificial intelligence, engineering, economics, and scientific inquiry; they are not only academic exercises. Learners acquire confidence in their ability to analyze mathematical models and comprehend the logic underlying algorithmic judgments by becoming proficient in equation manipulation.

Another key element that links algebra and artificial intelligence is patterns. Algebra is useful for finding patterns in geometric configurations, functional relationships, and numerical sequences. Because intelligent systems must identify significant structures within massive datasets, pattern recognition is at the core of machine learning. Instead of focusing on isolated observations, algebraic thinking teaches students to look for consistent correlations. When examining consumer behavior, financial trends, biological data, or linguistic patterns, this viewpoint is helpful. Algebra directly supports intelligent learning by enabling algorithms to generate predictions from previously seen data by recognizing mathematical regularities.

By expressing how one variable depends on another in accordance with a particular rule, functions expand algebra. A function takes one or more inputs and predictably generates matching outputs. Since almost all computational models can be thought of as collections of interrelated functions, this idea is fundamental to artificial intelligence. The system receives data as input, transforms it mathematically through several functions, and then generates recommendations, classifications, or predictions. Learners might see AI algorithms as methodical information mappings rather than as enigmatic computational processes when they understand their functions.

When researching machine learning, the link between inputs and outputs is very crucial. Algorithms search for functions that faithfully capture hidden patterns in data during training. Machine learning finds mathematical relationships that generalize to new scenarios rather than learning from every single example. An image recognition model, for example, trains a function that links object categories to numerical picture attributes. After learning this function, the model may use the same mathematical relationship to classify photos that have never been viewed before. What sets intelligent systems apart from straightforward lookup tables or rule-based programs is their capacity for generalization.

These relationships can be succinctly described using function notation. Mathematical notation like f(x) conveys that, in accordance with a predetermined rule, the output depends on the input. Even though the notation might seem strange at first, it provides exceptional precision and clarity. Researchers widely use function notation to describe statistical models, optimization processes, and machine learning algorithms. Students can read technical documents more confidently and comprehend the mathematical underpinnings of AI systems by learning to decipher this notation.

Within artificial intelligence, many functions have diverse functions. Relationships that vary at a constant rate are described by linear functions, which are frequently a helpful starting point for creating predictive models. More complicated behaviors that occur in real-world systems where changes are not proportionate are captured by nonlinear functions. Each of the functions—exponential, logarithmic, polynomial, and trigonometric—models' particular kinds of relationships seen in applications related to science, finance, and engineering. To approximate extremely complex patterns that would be impossible to express with basic equations alone, modern neural networks incorporate numerous nonlinear functions. Learners can better understand why specific mathematical models are selected for particular AI problems by comprehending the features of various function types.

Graphs offer visual depictions of functions that facilitate the interpretation of mathematical relationships. Trends, slopes, crossings, and general behavior can be seen by plotting inputs against outputs. Researchers can determine whether a relationship is linear, nonlinear, growing, decreasing, or periodic by using graphic analysis. Graphs are widely used in artificial intelligence to show data distributions, learning progress, prediction accuracy, and error reduction. By connecting abstract equations to intuitive geometric interpretations, the visualization of mathematical relationships helps students develop their analytical abilities and deepen their understanding.

Two key ideas related to functions are domain and range. While the range identifies potential outcomes, the domain defines the permitted input values. Gaining an understanding of these ideas helps define the capabilities and constraints of mathematical models. Artificial intelligence systems frequently operate within specific domains dictated by data availability or real-world constraints. For instance, a medical diagnosis model's outputs might include probabilities for various diagnoses, but it might accept only patient data gathered through authorized testing. Understanding the domain and range of functions contributes to the proper application and interpretation of models.

Function composition shows how basic mathematical relationships can come together to create complex behavior. Many AI systems use a series of interconnected functions to process information rather than depending on a single sophisticated function. Before sending its result to the next step, each function performs a specific transformation. This method is best demonstrated by neural networks, which combine multiple layers of mathematical functions to extract useful features from unprocessed data gradually. By understanding function composition, one can see how relatively simple mathematical procedures can cooperate systematically to produce complex intelligence.

By flipping mathematical relationships, inverse functions offer an additional insightful viewpoint. An inverse function tries to restore the original inputs from outputs that one function has transformed. Applications of inverse relationships in artificial intelligence include generative modeling, data reconstruction, image restoration, and encryption. Studying inverse functions improves comprehension of reversible transformations and mathematical reasoning, even though not all functions have a genuine inverse.

One of the most crucial steps in machine learning is optimization, which is greatly aided by algebra and functions. AI models continuously adjust their mathematical parameters during training to improve prediction accuracy. These modifications are based on algebraic formulas that explain how variations in variables affect overall performance. Algebra offers methods for effectively manipulating these mathematical relationships, whereas functions specify objective metrics that algorithms aim to maximize. Optimization techniques wouldn't have the structure required for methodical development without a strong grasp of algebra and functions.

The practical significance of these ideas is demonstrated via real-world applications. Recommendation systems evaluate consumer preferences based on past behavior using algebraic models and functions. To forecast market trends, financial forecasting uses the functional relationships between economic variables. Medical diagnostic systems analyze mathematical correlations between symptoms, test results, and patient histories.

Autonomous vehicles continuously assess functions describing speed, location, direction, and environmental variables. In each instance, functions and algebra provide the mathematical vocabulary that enables intelligent systems to convert raw data into insightful judgments.

Additionally, learning functions and algebra fosters more general analytical abilities that go beyond artificial intelligence. Equation solving promotes methodical problem solving, logical reasoning, and attention to detail. Working with functions improves one's capacity to identify trends, decipher connections, and forecast results using the information at hand. These mental skills are useful in numerous fields, including science, engineering, economics, and healthcare. The focused thinking that mathematics studies foster benefits even those who do not pursue careers in artificial intelligence.

Many students originally see algebra as abstract or unrelated to real-world applications. But as artificial intelligence shows, algebra is much more than just a subject for academics. Algebraic reasoning and functional relationships work behind the scenes in every voice assistant response, internet recommendation, mapping software-generated navigation route, and picture recognition system. Acknowledging these practical uses encourages students to delve deeper into the basic principles of mathematics and helps them understand their relevance.

Rather than relying solely on memorization, building solid foundations requires regular practice. Solving puzzles, investigating connections, deciphering graphs, and applying ideas to real-world situations all contribute to developing understanding. More complex subjects like linear algebra, calculus, probability, and optimization are increasingly supported by an interconnected framework that is built atop each new mathematical concept. A strong foundation for understanding machine learning, neural networks, and other advanced AI technologies is created by students who devote effort to mastering algebra and functions.

In the end, algebra and functions are much more than just basic mathematical concepts. They supply the vocabulary that artificial intelligence uses to model relationships, explain facts, and produce intelligent action. Complex real-world phenomena are transformed into structured mathematical forms that computers can effectively analyze using variables, equations, expressions, functions, and graphs. Instead of seeing AI systems as enigmatic technology, learners can understand the mathematical rationale behind them by building confidence in these fundamental ideas. In addition to preparing people for further education, this information enables them to actively engage in a future in which artificial intelligence will continue to impact almost every facet of industry, science, and society.

Developing Logical and Analytical Problem-Solving Skills

One of the most beneficial features of studying mathematics and artificial intelligence is the development of logical and analytical problem-solving skills. These abilities help people approach complicated problems methodically, assess the facts impartially, spot trends, and make wise decisions based on logic rather than conjecture. Since mathematical thinking and logical reasoning are the foundation of artificial intelligence, these skills are crucial for anyone trying to understand or build intelligent systems. Logical and analytical thinking is the cornerstone of successful problem-solving, whether one is tackling scientific topics, creating machine learning models, analyzing corporate data, or overcoming programming challenges. By developing these abilities, students are better able to comprehend complex material, find effective solutions, and successfully adapt to novel technical challenges.

The capacity for methodical, consistent reasoning is known as logical thinking. Instead of relying on assumptions or feelings, it makes inferences from the information at hand, following precise guidelines. Every logical argument consists of a series of related concepts with prior evidence to support each conclusion. Logical reasoning is used in mathematics to validate answers, simplify equations, and establish theorems. Similar concepts are used by artificial intelligence to assess circumstances, forecast outcomes, and choose the best course of action. Logical reasoning guarantees that intelligent systems consistently process information and generate trustworthy results depending on the data at hand.

By emphasizing meticulous data analysis, analytical thinking enhances logical reasoning. Analytical thinking breaks down a problem into smaller, more manageable components that can be examined separately rather than as a single, overwhelming challenge. This procedure aids in identifying connections, crucial information, and removing superfluous complexity. Artificial intelligence systems conduct similar studies by examining by examining several features in datasets, measuring correlations between variables, and identifying patterns that enable precise predictions. Thus, analytical thinking offers a methodical way to comprehend issues before attempting to resolve them.

The first step in tackling a problem is to define it precisely. Many problems occur because the real issue has not been accurately diagnosed, not because there are no answers. Gathering information, defining goals, recognizing limitations, and comprehending the variables affecting the situation are the initial steps taken by effective problem solvers. This similar idea is applied by artificial intelligence when it comes to data preparation, where algorithms find pertinent variables, arrange data, and eliminate inconsistencies before learning starts. A well-defined problem establishes a solid basis for effective analysis and decision-making.

Another crucial method of problem-solving is to divide complicated issues into smaller parts. When viewed in their entirety, large difficulties can seem daunting, but they are easier to examine and resolve when broken down into smaller, more manageable chunks. This idea is commonly used in computer science through modular programming, which builds huge software systems as collections of smaller functions. Similarly, complex tasks are processed by artificial intelligence systems by breaking them into several computational phases. This methodical breakdown increases comprehension while lowering the possibility of missing crucial information.

Logical and analytical thinking heavily relies on the ability to recognize patterns. Once recurrent structures or relationships are found, many issues become simpler to address. Students learn to identify algebraic structures, geometric correlations, and numerical patterns in mathematics that make computations easier. By using machine learning algorithms to extract patterns from massive datasets, artificial intelligence expands on this idea. Language models discover grammatical structures, image recognition systems uncover visual patterns, and recommendation systems find commonalities among consumer preferences. Both humans and intelligent systems can make predictions and solve problems more effectively when they can identify patterns.

Another crucial element of analytical problem-solving is reasoning via evidence. Rather than being based on conjecture or personal prejudice, effective decisions should be backed by facts, observations, and logical analysis. By calculating probabilities, measuring relationships, and assessing uncertainty, statistical techniques aid in evaluating evidence. Because machine learning models enhance their performance by learning from observed data rather than adhering to preset assumptions, artificial intelligence primarily relies on evidence-based learning. This focus on objective evidence encourages more trustworthy decision-making and more accurate conclusions.

By encouraging people to thoroughly consider the facts before concluding, critical thinking enhances logical problem-solving. Critical thinkers look at supporting data, spot any flaws, and take into account other explanations rather than assuming that every statement is true. Artificial intelligence researchers use similar logic to evaluate algorithms, assess machine learning models, and validate experimental findings. By ensuring that judgments are based on thorough investigation rather than on insufficient data or unproven assumptions, critical thinking reduces errors.

Another crucial ability acquired via artificial intelligence and mathematics is abstraction. Abstraction identifies broad principles that hold across a variety of circumstances rather than focusing solely on particular instances. Computational models, algorithms, and mathematical formulas are abstract descriptions that can solve entire classes of issues rather than individual cases. Abstraction is highly beneficial to artificial intelligence, as learning algorithms can generalize to previously unseen data by identifying general patterns. This capacity for generalization sets intelligent learning apart from rote memorizing.

Making decisions in the face of ambiguity is yet another crucial component of analytical reasoning. Complete information is rarely available in real-world scenarios; people and intelligent systems must make decisions in the face of uncertainty. By estimating expected outcomes and calculating confidence levels, probability theory and statistics provide mathematical techniques for assessing ambiguous situations. These ideas are used by artificial intelligence in picture recognition, illness diagnosis, financial trend prediction, and unknown environment navigation. Even when full certainty is unattainable, intelligent systems can make well-informed decisions by combining probabilistic thinking with logical reasoning.

Algorithms show how logical thought can be converted into methodical problem-solving processes. An algorithm is a series of precisely defined processes that reliably yield the intended outcome. Algorithms are used in routine tasks like following a recipe or building furniture, while computer programs carry out much more intricate computational processes. Algorithms for learning, optimization, classification, and prediction play a major role in artificial intelligence. Learners can organize their logical reasoning into effective methods for tackling increasingly complex issues by studying algorithms.

An outstanding illustration of analytical problem-solving in action is debugging. Sometimes, logical mistakes, missing data, or unforeseen circumstances cause software programs and machine learning models to generate inaccurate findings. Until the fundamental issue is identified, debugging requires meticulous observation, methodical testing, and the rational exclusion of potential causes. Debugging requires evidence-based reasoning and methodical analysis rather than haphazard guesswork. Beyond computer science, these same analytical abilities are useful in many other fields.

By challenging problem solvers to choose the optimal option from a variety of options, optimization enhances logical reasoning. Optimization problems involving resource allocation, scheduling, route planning, and parameter adjustment are often resolved using artificial intelligence. Optimization algorithms balance conflicting goals and constraints while systematically evaluating a wide range of options. This mathematical method shows that addressing problems often entails refining existing answers rather than merely identifying a workable option. Analytical and logical thinking is also beneficial for collaboration. Teams of people with varying backgrounds and specialties frequently contribute to complex undertakings. Clear explanations of concepts, constructive challenges to presumptions, and the use of facts rather than subjective judgment to settle disputes are all made possible by logical communication. Collaboration amongst mathematicians, computer scientists, engineers, domain specialists, and designers is often necessary for the development of artificial intelligence. Strong analytical abilities foster effective communication and clear reasoning, which enhances teamwork.

Real-world applications emphasize how crucial logical and analytical problem-solving is. Before making a diagnosis, medical experts examine medical histories, test results, and symptoms. Engineers assess design options while taking cost, efficiency, and safety into account. Before making investing decisions, financial analysts evaluate economic indicators and market movements. To comprehend long-term trends, environmental scientists examine climate data. By analyzing large amounts of data, identifying trends, and generating recommendations based on solid evidence, artificial intelligence helps these professionals. However, the efficacy of these systems relies on the logical ideas ingrained in their mathematical underpinnings.

The importance of methodical reasoning is continuously demonstrated by artificial intelligence itself. By repeatedly analyzing training data, machine learning models get better at predicting outcomes with ever-higher accuracy. Natural language processing systems interpret sentences by analyzing contextual relationships and grammatical structures. To identify objects across a variety of settings, computer vision algorithms analyze visual characteristics. Analytical thinking and logical reasoning guide the conversion of raw data into useful knowledge across every application.

Gaining these abilities also promotes lifelong learning. As technology advances quickly, new tools, programming languages, and artificial intelligence methods are introduced. Strong logical and analytical skills enable people to adjust more readily, as they understand the underlying principles rather than relying solely on methods committed to memory. These fundamental cognitive abilities facilitate ongoing education, innovative problem-solving, and sound decision-making in ever- changing work settings.

In conclusion, understanding mathematics, artificial intelligence, and contemporary technology requires developing logical, analytical problem-solving skills. Analytical thinking enables the methodical exploration of complex issues and the identification of effective solutions, while logical reasoning provides structured approaches to reaching trustworthy findings. Pattern identification, abstraction, evidence-based reasoning, critical thinking, algorithmic design, debugging, and optimization are just a few of the skills that equip students to tackle problems in a variety of fields. These ideas are embodied in artificial intelligence through data analysis, the identification of meaningful relationships, and decision-making in the face of ambiguity. Strong logical and analytical problem-solving abilities will continue to be essential for creativity, responsible decision-making, and successful engagement in an increasingly data-driven world as intelligent technologies continue to impact science, engineering, healthcare, finance, education, and daily life.

Connecting Mathematical Concepts to Intelligent Systems

Understanding how artificial intelligence works and develops requires making the connection between mathematical ideas and intelligent systems. The actual potential of AI applications lies in mathematics, even though they often seem to rely primarily on complex software or powerful hardware. Mathematical principles govern the behavior of all intelligent systems, be they speech recognition, image classification, financial trend prediction, or product recommendations. Mathematics provides the language for expressing knowledge, the instruments for examining relationships, and the strategies for enhancing decision-making over time. Learners gain insight into how machines convert raw input into meaningful information and how intelligent technologies tackle ever more complex challenges by understanding these mathematical foundations.

Through information processing, pattern recognition, prediction, and experience-based learning, intelligent systems are made to mimic some characteristics of human reasoning. But unlike people, computers cannot rely on intuition or firsthand knowledge to understand the environment. Before any observation can be analyzed, it must first be represented mathematically. Spoken language is transformed into digital signals, written text is represented by mathematical vectors that reflect word relationships, and images are transformed into collections of numerical values corresponding to pixels. No matter what kind of data is being examined, computers can execute mathematical operations consistently and effectively thanks to this numerical representation. One of the key traits of intelligent systems is their capacity to transform various types of data into mathematical structures.

One of the first mathematical links to artificial intelligence is algebra. Changes in quantities and relationships can be represented in various ways using variables, equations, and expressions. Intelligent systems use variables to characterize prediction outputs, model parameters modified during learning, and features extracted from data. The interactions among these variables are defined by algebraic equations, which enable algorithms to convert inputs into useful outputs. To determine which products are most likely to be of interest to a specific user, a recommendation system might, for instance, employ algebraic connections to combine client preferences, purchase history, and product features. These correlations would be challenging to articulate and far more challenging to compute effectively without algebra.

By defining exact mappings between inputs and outputs, functions expand algebra. All intelligent systems perform a series of operations that transform raw data into forecasts or judgments. These changes are mathematical operations that follow well-defined guidelines. Finding functions that faithfully capture patterns in training data is the goal of machine learning. These functions can be applied to fresh data once they have been learned, enabling AI systems to generalize beyond training instances. Intelligent systems use mathematical operations to link observed data with intended results, whether they be interpreting languages, identifying handwritten numbers, or spotting fraudulent transactions.

Because large sets of numerical values are often processed simultaneously by modern artificial intelligence systems, linear algebra offers yet another important framework. While matrices arrange several observations into structured patterns appropriate for calculation, vectors organize individual observations. Before being fed into machine learning algorithms, images, documents, audio recordings, and sensor measurements are all transformed into vectors or matrices. By using standardized operations, these mathematical structures enable computers to perform millions of calculations efficiently. Because linear algebra provides the computational foundation for handling high-dimensional data, neural networks, recommendation systems, and natural language processing models all rely heavily on it.

By offering methods for visualizing relationships between data points, geometry adds more understanding to intelligent systems. Machine learning frequently uses multidimensional spaces to describe information, with each observation occupying a distinct place based on its attributes. Different observations stay farther apart, while similar observations appear closer together. Distance, direction, angles, and borders are examples of geometric concepts that help explain how algorithms detect similarities, identify clusters, and define categories. For instance, by creating mathematical boundaries that separate various objects in high-dimensional feature spaces, image classification models classify images. The basic mathematical concepts are nonetheless closely related, even if these spaces go well beyond standard three-dimensional geometry.

Another significant mathematical link is calculus, since intelligent systems get better by continuously adjusting internal parameters. Prediction mistakes are measured by machine learning algorithms, which then steadily minimize them by altering mathematical relationships. Calculus offers derivatives that explain how little adjustments affect overall performance, enabling optimization techniques to identify the path toward improvement. This process is crucial to training neural networks, which update millions of parameters through repeated computations until predictions become more accurate. Therefore, rather than staying fixed after initial programming, calculus allows intelligent systems to learn from experience.

One of the most useful uses of mathematics in intelligent systems is optimization. Each AI model aims to accomplish particular goals, such as increasing computational efficiency, reducing classification errors, or optimizing prediction accuracy. By modifying mathematical parameters in accordance with goal functions, optimization techniques methodically look for better solutions. Intelligent systems don't rely on haphazard experimentation; instead, they adhere to meticulously planned optimization processes that direct learning toward ever-more-effective models. Optimization is one of the key mechanisms underpinning adaptive intelligence, as it enables AI applications to improve as they encounter more data over time.

Since uncertainty is present in almost all real-world issues, probability is essential. Incomplete knowledge, unclear circumstances, measurement errors, and unforeseen events are all present in human contexts. Therefore, rather than waiting for flawless information, intelligent systems must make decisions in the face of uncertainty. Based on the facts at hand, probability provides numerical methods for estimating the likelihood of various scenarios. Recommendation engines estimate the likelihood that consumers will love specific products, autonomous vehicles assess the possibility of obstacles, and medical diagnosis systems estimate the probability of diseases. Instead of assuming total certainty, these probabilistic computations enable AI systems to function efficiently while accepting ambiguity.

By enabling intelligent systems to learn from data, statistics improves the accuracy of probability estimates. Statistical techniques assist researchers in comprehending dataset properties, spotting trends, quantifying variability, and assessing data quality before training. Statistics offers methods for evaluating performance, comparing algorithms, and assessing the significance of observed advances during model development. Instead of learning random fluctuations from training data, statistical reasoning guarantees that intelligent systems recognize real correlations. This thorough analysis validates models that can effectively generalize to previously unforeseen scenarios.

Because computers process discrete data rather than continuous data, discrete mathematics creates another crucial link. Many AI applications that deal with relationships among objects rather than straightforward numerical computations are supported by concepts such as graph theory, logic, sets, and combinatorics. By establishing mathematical connections between items, graph topologies depict social networks, transportation networks, communication networks, and biological interactions. Discrete mathematical concepts are used by knowledge graphs, search algorithms, and recommendation systems to organize data and identify meaningful relationships effectively. These structures show how various fields of mathematics must cooperate harmoniously for intelligent systems to function.

The framework for reasoning that underpins intelligent conduct is provided by logic. All AI algorithms adhere to logical guidelines that dictate how data should be analyzed and conclusions should be drawn. By defining uniform norms for assessing conditions and making judgments, mathematical logic removes ambiguity. Logical frameworks are essential to rule-based AI, expert systems, and automated reasoning applications. By adhering to scientifically defined optimization processes and decision criteria, even machine learning models subtly contain logical thinking. Gaining an understanding of logic enables students to recognize that intelligent systems operate through systematic reasoning rather than erratic intuition.

Another crucial mathematical relationship is demonstrated by data representation. Seldom is raw data from sensors, documents, photos, or databases available in formats that can be computed directly. Mathematical techniques convert raw data into structured representations that allow for effective analysis while maintaining key features. Vector embeddings, dimensionality reduction, and feature extraction all rely on mathematical principles that simplify complex data without sacrificing important information. Since algorithms can only examine patterns found in their mathematical formulations, effective data representation frequently determines the success of intelligent systems.

Pattern recognition shows how several mathematical ideas interact in artificial intelligence. By integrating algebra, geometry, statistics, and optimization into cohesive computational frameworks, intelligent systems can recognize recurring structures. Facial recognition systems, for instance, evaluate numerical representations of images, compute feature-vector similarities, use statistical models to estimate probabilities, and optimize decision boundaries that separate different people. Each branch of mathematics adds specific tools, but when applied together, they create intelligent behavior that is far more potent than any one idea working alone.

The concept of machine learning itself is an amalgam of many mathematical concepts that collaborate to achieve shared goals. Calculus facilitates optimization, algebra defines relationships between variables, functions provide predictive mappings, probability quantifies uncertainty, statistics assesses learning, and linear algebra allows for effective computation. Throughout the learning process, these mathematical disciplines support one another rather than existing as discrete subjects. Learners can see that artificial intelligence is essentially an interdisciplinary mathematical endeavor rather than just a programming exercise by understanding its interconnected responsibilities.

Real-world applications demonstrate how crucial it is to link mathematics to intelligent systems. Mathematical models are used in healthcare to evaluate medical imaging, forecast disease progression, and customize therapies. To identify fraud and control investment risk, financial organizations use probability, optimization, and statistical learning. Intelligent systems are used in manufacturing for process optimization, predictive maintenance, and quality control. While transportation depends on mathematical algorithms to direct autonomous cars and optimize traffic flow, agriculture benefits from AI's analysis of environmental data to increase crop yields. Every example demonstrates how mathematical ideas directly impact technical solutions that tackle real-world problems.

The need for interpretability has grown as intelligent systems impact crucial decisions. Understanding mathematics enables researchers to assess algorithmic fairness, determine influential variables, and examine why models generate specific results. In AI applications, transparent mathematical frameworks aid in identifying biases, evaluating dependability, and enhancing accountability. Mathematical reasoning clarifies algorithms' inherent structure and decision-making processes, encouraging trust and prudent implementation in delicate fields, rather than viewing them as enigmatic black boxes.

Mathematical knowledge is also necessary for ethical considerations. Artificial intelligence systems affect criminal justice procedures, employment decisions, loan approvals, healthcare recommendations, and educational prospects. Unintentional biases in datasets can be identified, population fairness can be assessed, and prediction uncertainty can be quantified using mathematical analysis. To create AI responsibly, it is necessary to strike a balance between ethical ideals and technical performance, proving that mathematics contributes to both computing efficiency and well-informed decision-making on societal impacts.

It takes constant work and curiosity to learn how to relate mathematical ideas to intelligent systems. Students gain from investigating how various mathematical concepts work together to solve practical issues rather than memorizing formulas on their own. By showcasing immediate applications, computer experiments, interdisciplinary initiatives, and real-world examples, computer experiments enhance conceptual understanding. As their understanding expands, students begin to identify recurring mathematical patterns that underlie seemingly unrelated AI systems, boosting their confidence and prompting further investigation.

In the end, applying mathematical ideas to intelligent systems shows that artificial intelligence is essentially a mathematical achievement rooted in centuries of intellectual advancement. The fundamental concepts that enable machines to analyze information, learn from experience, and make sound judgments are provided by algebra, functions, geometry, linear algebra, calculus, probability, statistics, optimization, logic, and discrete mathematics. These interrelated fields provide the accuracy, consistency, and analytical capacity required for intelligent action while converting unprocessed data into useful knowledge. People who understand these mathematical connections will be better equipped to assess new technologies, develop creative solutions, and contribute responsibly to future advancements as artificial intelligence continues to spread across science, business, healthcare, education, and daily life. Learners acquire the skills and self-assurance necessary to contribute significantly to the ongoing development of intelligent systems and the revolutionary potential they bring to society by developing solid mathematical foundations and comprehending their real-world applications.

CHAPTER II
Linear Algebra and Geometry for Intelligent Computing

Vectors, Matrices, and Transformations

Among the most crucial mathematical ideas underpinning robotics, computer graphics, artificial intelligence, machine learning, engineering, and data science are vectors, matrices, and transformations. These ideas fall within the field of linear algebra, which provides the mathematical foundation for handling and representing large amounts of numerical data. To organize data, perform computations, and extract meaningful patterns from complex datasets, contemporary artificial intelligence systems rely heavily on vectors and matrices. Intelligent systems constantly perform mathematical operations involving vectors, matrices, and transformations, whether they are used for image recognition, language translation, product recommendation, or autonomous vehicle control. Gaining an understanding of these ideas helps students understand how artificial intelligence conveys information, efficiently analyzes data, and carries out complex calculations that facilitate wise decision-making.

An ordered set of numbers that represents a quantity with several components is called a vector. A vector can describe multiple linked measurements at once, in contrast to a single numerical value. Vectors are frequently shown as rows or columns of numbers in mathematics. Vectors are used in artificial intelligence to represent data features, such as an image's qualities, a customer's attributes, or the meaning of a sentence's words. A music recommendation system might use a vector that describes the tempo, rhythm, genre, and other features of each song. In contrast, a photograph might be represented as a long vector containing the numerical values of its pixels. Intelligent systems can effectively compare, analyze, and interpret complex data by representing information as vectors.

In geometry, vectors are important for defining movement and spatial relationships because they have both magnitude and direction. Vectors are used in physics to represent forces, accelerations, and velocities. Vectors are used in robotics to describe the position and motion of autonomous vehicles or robotic arms. Similar ideas are used by artificial intelligence to navigate real settings and analyze object locations within photographs. The mathematical properties of vectors remain unchanged, even though many machine learning applications focus on numerical attributes rather than physical motion. These characteristics offer a uniform vocabulary for characterizing multidimensional data in a variety of fields.

Machine learning relies heavily on vector operations. While scalar multiplication modifies a vector's size by multiplying each component by the same numerical value, vector addition combines corresponding components of two vectors. The dot product, which measures the similarity between two vectors by multiplying their components and summing the results, is another crucial operation. The dot product is widely used in artificial intelligence to compute neural network outputs, compare documents, and assess visual similarity. This method is crucial for natural language processing, recommendation systems, and search engines because larger dot products frequently show stronger associations between vectors.

By arranging several vectors into rectangular rows and columns, matrices expand on the idea of vectors. A complete dataset can be represented by a matrix, with each row denoting an observation and each column denoting a feature. For instance, a client database might be set up as a matrix with thousands of people's ages, incomes, geographic locations, and shopping preferences. In a similar vein, matrices can be used to represent digital photos, financial information, scientific measurements, and sensor readings. Computers can efficiently perform large-scale computations while preserving consistency across various data types thanks to this organization.

Many algorithms for artificial intelligence are based on matrix operations. Scalar multiplication and matrix addition operate on similar principles as vectors, but matrix multiplication is particularly important since it allows for intricate data manipulations. In matrix multiplication, specific mathematical rules govern how rows of one matrix interact with columns of another to produce a new matrix that incorporates data from both. Because these operations efficiently handle large amounts of numerical data, neural networks perform billions of matrix multiplications during training and prediction. Because matrix computations are crucial to artificial intelligence, specialized computer hardware, such as graphics processing units, has been developed specifically to accelerate them.

Another key idea in linear algebra is the identity matrix. When multiplied correctly, the identity matrix leaves other matrices unaltered, just like the number one in regular multiplication. Because of this mathematical property, the identity matrix can be used to solve systems of equations, analyze transformations, and implement computer algorithms. Identity matrices are frequently used in artificial intelligence applications to initialize computations or streamline mathematical processes during model construction.

Another useful mathematical tool is matrix inversion. When a matrix has an inverse, the impact of the original matrix under multiplication is reversed. In statistical analysis, machine learning techniques, optimization, and the solution of systems of linear equations are crucial. Artificial intelligence systems can compute inverses of large matrices when needed, thanks to efficient numerical techniques, even though doing so can be computationally taxing. Learners can better realize how mathematical relationships can be systematically reversed or reconstructed by comprehending matrix inversion.

Transformations are mathematical procedures that modify vectors and matrices. Transformations in geometry include scaling, shearing, rotation, translation, and reflection. These operations alter an object's size, position, or orientation while maintaining crucial structural relationships. By transforming data representations, artificial intelligence expands these concepts beyond physical geometry. Machine learning algorithms convert numerical information into forms that facilitate the recognition and analysis of patterns rather than just changing shapes.

Because they maintain basic mathematical relationships, linear transformations are particularly significant. A linear transformation preserves addition and scalar multiplication features while mapping one vector space into another. Computers can perform complex modifications using effective numerical calculations thanks to matrix multiplication, which offers a practical mathematical representation of linear transformations. As information moves through successive layers, neural networks continuously apply linear transformations, progressively extracting increasingly significant patterns from the incoming data.

One of the most useful uses of linear algebra in machine learning is feature transformation. Unnecessary complexity or variables that are difficult to analyze directly are common in raw data. These original features are transformed mathematically into new representations that make learning easier and increase prediction accuracy. For instance, principal component analysis preserves most of the original data while decomposing correlated variables into smaller sets of independent components. Machine learning models can analyze data more effectively and use less computing power thanks to these modified features.

Another significant use of vectors, matrices, and transformations is seen in computer graphics. Vectors that describe the positions of an object's vertices represent three-dimensional objects, while transformation matrices govern rotation, scaling, and translation in virtual environments. These mathematical procedures are used to create realistic visual experiences in video games, animated movies, virtual reality systems, and engineering simulations. By fusing machine learning with geometric transformations to produce increasingly complex visual effects and interactive settings, artificial intelligence is making a significant contribution to computer graphics.

Linear algebra is also essential to robotics. When dealing with physical environments, robotic systems must precisely determine their locations, orientations, and movements. Robotic arms, driverless cars, and industrial automation equipment may all be precisely controlled thanks to transformation matrices, which describe the motion of robotic joints and coordinate systems. By fusing sensor data with mathematical models that enable navigation, object recognition, and decision-making in dynamic environments, artificial intelligence enhances robotic capabilities.

Another intriguing use of vectors and transformations is in natural language processing. Words, phrases, and sentences are represented by numerical vectors called embeddings in contemporary language models. To place words with comparable meanings, close together in mathematical space, these vectors encode semantic associations. Neural networks can examine these correlations, comprehend context, and produce meaningful responses thanks to transformation matrices. Information retrieval, text summarization, conversational artificial intelligence, and machine translation have all been transformed by this mathematical model.

Vectors and matrices are also used in image recognition systems. Grids of numerical pixel values, naturally represented as matrices, make up digital images. To extract features such as edges, textures, shapes, and objects, neural networks repeatedly modify these matrices through successive computational layers. Until the system can identify intricate visual patterns, each change reveals progressively more abstract information. This multi-layered method shows how mathematical modifications allow artificial intelligence to interpret visual data accurately.

Additionally, learning about vectors, matrices, and transformations enhances more general mathematical reasoning. Students gain the ability to see patterns in space, think abstractly, solve computational problems, and understand how mathematical ideas relate to one another. Beyond artificial intelligence, these abilities are useful in engineering, economics, physics, architecture, biology, and many other scientific fields where mathematical modeling and multidimensional data are crucial.

In conclusion, the mathematical foundation of many computing technologies and contemporary artificial intelligence consists of vectors, matrices, and transformations. Transformations alter data in ways that reveal significant patterns; matrices organize massive datasets and enable powerful computations; and vectors offer effective representations of complex information. Intelligent systems can process images, comprehend language, navigate environments, and make precise predictions thanks to matrix multiplication, linear transformations, feature extraction, geometric operations, and multidimensional representations. The concepts of linear algebra will remain essential for creating intelligent systems that can effectively, precisely, and reliably solve increasingly complex real-world problems as artificial intelligence advances across a variety of industries, including healthcare, finance, education, transportation, scientific research, and many more.

Systems of Linear Equations and Matrix Operations

Among the most crucial mathematical ideas behind artificial intelligence, data science, engineering, economics, and many other scientific fields are systems of linear equations and matrix operations. These subjects are useful tools for expressing relationships between variables and performing efficient computations on large datasets, even though they are often presented in standard mathematics courses as abstract methods for solving for unknown values. Systems of linear equations and matrix operations are crucial for organizing information, modeling relationships, optimizing algorithms, and processing data since many artificial intelligence problems need the simultaneous analysis of numerous variables. Gaining a solid grasp of these ideas helps students understand how mathematical reasoning underpins intelligent systems that can solve increasingly challenging real-world problems.

A linear equation is one in which all variables are mixed by addition, subtraction, or multiplication by constants and appear only to the first power. These equations represent straight-line relationships between variables, which makes them incredibly helpful even though they are relatively easy to evaluate. A single linear equation may represent one relationship, but many real-world issues involve multiple variables interacting at once. In these circumstances, a set of equations referred to as a system of linear equations offers a mathematical model that explains how various quantities affect one another. Because real-world datasets rarely rely on a single variable, artificial intelligence often encounters these interrelated interactions.

Numerous commonplace circumstances naturally lead to systems of linear equations. To assess profitability, a company may look at material, labor, and production costs. Transportation planners can calculate travel times between connected routes. While economists study the relationships among markets, supply, and demand, engineers may assess the forces acting on structures. By simulating relationships among features in datasets, artificial intelligence broadens these applications. For instance, factors reflecting location, size, age, number of rooms, and neighborhood features might be taken into account by a machine learning system forecasting house values. Mathematical interactions between these variables create systems that explain how various factors influence expected results.

Finding solutions that satisfy all equations simultaneously is one of the main objectives when working with systems of linear equations. A solution is a set of variable values that satisfy all of the system's relationships. A system may have a single solution, an unlimited number of solutions, or no solution at all, depending on how the equations are structured. Knowing these possibilities makes it easier for students to understand that, for mathematical models to yield meaningful results, they must accurately represent real-world circumstances. Similarly, artificial intelligence relies on finding suitable mathematical models that best describe observed facts while adhering to existing evidence.

Systems of linear equations can be solved using a variety of techniques. Substitution and elimination are two conventional methods that progressively reduce complexity until unknown variables can be identified. While elimination combines equations to remove specific variables, substitution uses information from another equation to substitute one variable. By showing how systematic mathematical procedures can simplify complicated situations, these approaches demonstrate logical reasoning. Even though manual computations are rarely used in modern artificial intelligence, these fundamental methods help students understand the logic underlying more complex algorithms.

Solving equations one at a time becomes ineffective as systems get bigger and more complicated. Traditional problem-solving techniques are impractical because artificial intelligence frequently examines datasets with dozens or millions of variables. By arranging systems of linear equations into small mathematical structures that computers can effectively handle, matrix representation solves this problem. Matrices provide structured representations appropriate for computational analysis by organizing coefficients into rows and columns rather than writing long collections of equations. One of the most important developments in mathematical computing is the shift from equations to matrices, which enables large-scale computations that would otherwise take a very long time.

A rectangular arrangement of numbers arranged into rows and columns is called a matrix. Within the original system of equations, each number has a defined place that represents a certain relationship. Matrices enable the effective implementation of computing algorithms while simplifying mathematical notation. Datasets, neural network parameters, image pixels, statistical models, and many other types of structured data are represented by matrices in artificial intelligence. Matrices provide a perfect foundation for managing large amounts of mathematical data, since computers naturally interpret ordered numerical arrays.

A system of linear equations can be transformed into matrix form to improve computation efficiency while maintaining all necessary information. While constants appear independently in the accompanying vectors, the coefficients of the variables form the entries of the matrix. Regardless of the particular problem being tackled, computers may use standardized algorithms thanks to this structured representation. As a result, matrix notation functions as a universal mathematical language that can describe a wide range of applications in fields such as science, engineering, physics, economics, and artificial intelligence.

One of the most basic operations on matrices is matrix addition. When comparable elements are combined separately, two matrices of the same dimensions can be added. This operation supports many computing tasks in artificial intelligence, despite its simplicity. Model parameters are often updated using machine learning techniques by adding adjustment matrices computed during optimization. While computer graphics incorporate modifications through repetitive matrix additions, statistical studies integrate data from several datasets. An understanding of matrix addition reinforces the significance of well-organized mathematical frameworks for effective computation.

By comparing matching elements between two matrices, matrix subtraction adheres to similar principles. This process computes parameter updates during machine learning, assesses prediction mistakes, and quantifies dataset differences. Artificial intelligence systems generate error matrices that direct further learning by continuously comparing expected values with observed results. Therefore, matrix subtraction directly contributes to the adaptive behavior that characterizes intelligent systems capable of gradually improving their performance.

One of the most crucial operations in linear algebra is matrix multiplication, which is far more complex. In contrast to regular multiplication, matrix multiplication uses well-defined mathematical rules to mix rows from one matrix with columns from another. Relationships that have been simultaneously transformed across several variables are described in the resulting matrix. Neural networks, recommendation systems, computer vision models, and language processing algorithms all carry out several matrix multiplications during training and prediction, making this operation crucial to artificial intelligence. Even when processing massive datasets, matrix multiplication maintains computing efficiency while enabling complicated mathematical manipulations.

Because identity matrices work similarly to the number one in regular arithmetic, they have a unique function within matrix operations. An identity matrix has zeros elsewhere and ones along its main diagonal. The original matrix remains unaltered when any compatible matrix is multiplied by an identity matrix. Identity matrices are widely used in theoretical investigations, numerical techniques, and optimization algorithms that underpin artificial intelligence. They offer reliable mathematical benchmarks that facilitate computations and enhance computational consistency.

By switching rows and columns, transpose operations reorganize matrices. Despite its seeming simplicity, this transformation has significant uses in data analysis and artificial intelligence. Matrix transposition makes it easier to compare datasets, supports optimization processes, and improves the efficiency of statistical computations. Training techniques for neural networks propagate information both forward and backward through layers of computation by repeatedly transposing matrices. Understanding transpose operations demonstrates how rearranging mathematical structures can frequently improve computational efficiency without changing the underlying data.

Another useful mathematical idea that is directly related to solving systems of linear equations is provided by inverse matrices. When a matrix has an inverse, multiplying it by that inverse yields the identity matrix, so it undoes the initial transformation. The fundamental idea of explicit matrix inversion remains crucial for understanding numerical techniques and solving mathematical models, even though it is not always feasible for large-scale artificial intelligence applications. To increase computer efficiency while maintaining mathematical accuracy, several optimization methods approximate inverse operations.

One of the most popular techniques for solving systems of linear equations using matrix operations is Gaussian elimination. This algorithm uses carefully selected row operations to systematically reduce matrices to simpler forms. The converted matrix eventually becomes simple to understand, making it possible to determine unknown variables effectively. Gaussian elimination is a crucial forerunner to contemporary computing algorithms used in artificial intelligence because it shows how logical mathematical processes can replace tedious human computations.

Matrix operations also support geometric transformations such as rotation, scaling, reflection, and translation. These changes are essential to robotics, computer graphics, and computer vision. Despite variations in orientation, size, or perspective, artificial intelligence systems that analyze photos sometimes modify visual information to enhance recognition. An elegant mathematical framework for reliably performing these geometric operations on large sets of visual data is provided by matrix multiplication. Gaining an understanding of these transformations shows how abstract mathematical procedures result in useful computational capabilities.

There are several instances of matrix operations and systems of linear equations cooperating in machine learning. By solving systems that describe observed data, linear regression models estimate relationships between variables. Classification methods use matrix computations to determine decision boundaries. Neural networks arrange millions of modifiable parameters into matrices that are often changed during optimization. Recommendation systems use matrix representations to compare product attributes and user preferences. Systems of linear equations provide mathematical models for these applications, and matrix operations facilitate efficient computation.

Their role in data representation further illustrates the significance of matrices in artificial intelligence. Each dataset is made up of features and observations that are naturally arranged into rows and columns. Usually, one observation is represented by each row, while each column represents a certain attribute. Instead of analyzing individual observations, algorithms can evaluate enormous datasets at once using matrix notation. This ability to process data in parallel greatly speeds up learning while making mathematical analysis easier. The importance of linear algebra in modern computing is evident in AI frameworks designed to leverage efficient matrix computations on specialized hardware.

To improve model performance, optimization techniques heavily rely on matrix operations and systems of linear equations. Algorithms repeatedly compute parameter updates during machine learning to reduce prediction errors. These updates frequently entail large-scale matrix multiplications or the solution of linear systems. With reasonable processing costs, intelligent systems can learn from millions of examples thanks to efficient optimization. Advanced neural network training might take unreasonably large calculation times without matrix-based optimization approaches.

Another interesting application is computer vision. Matrix representations of pixel intensities across various color channels make up digital images. Matrix operations are used regularly in processing pipelines for image enhancement, feature extraction, edge detection, and object recognition. One of the most effective AI designs for image recognition is the convolutional neural network, which relies almost entirely on efficient matrix operations. Each identified object, identified face, or categorized medical image is the outcome of several matrix operations that convert unprocessed pixel input into useful representations.

Similarly, matrices that encode words, phrases, and contextual relationships are essential to natural language processing. Semantic data is represented using word embeddings as high-dimensional vectors stored in matrices. While producing logical answers, translating languages, and responding to inquiries, language models carry out lengthy matrix multiplications. While matrix operations enable effective learning from massive text collections with billions of words, systems of equations capture correlations among linguistic traits.

Systems of linear equations and matrix operations are useful in scientific research, engineering, economics, healthcare, and environmental modeling. Climate scientists use interrelated equations to model atmospheric interactions. Engineers use matrix methods to study structural stability. To enhance disease detection, medical experts use mathematical processing of diagnostic data. Economists use systems that describe the links between financial variables to predict market behavior. By fusing mathematical modeling with adaptive learning, artificial intelligence expands these capabilities and makes forecasts in a variety of fields more accurate.

Studying matrix operations and systems of linear equations also improves more general analytical abilities. By utilizing structured techniques to solve complex issues, identifying links between variables, and methodically organizing information, learners acquire logical reasoning. While solving equations fosters perseverance, accuracy, and mathematical confidence, matrix thinking promotes effective organization of information. Beyond artificial intelligence, these cognitive skills remain useful across a wide range of scientific, technological, and professional domains.

In the end, systems of linear equations and matrix operations provide the fundamental mathematical underpinnings of contemporary computer research and intelligent systems. They facilitate prediction, optimization, pattern identification, and data analysis while converting intricate relationships into well-organized mathematical structures that computers can interpret well. These ideas may be found in almost every field of artificial intelligence, from representing information and training neural networks to evaluating images and comprehending language. Learners acquire the skills required to comprehend how intelligent technologies carry out complex computations, adapt through learning, and resolve real-world issues impacting science, business, healthcare, education, and daily life by mastering systems of linear equations and matrix operations. The power of artificial intelligence ultimately rests upon well-developed foundations of logical reasoning and linear algebra, since these mathematical principles continue to propel innovation.

Geometry in High-Dimensional Data Representation

One of the key mathematical ideas underpinning contemporary artificial intelligence is geometry in high-dimensional data representation. Geometry's concepts extend well beyond the real world, even though it is typically associated with shapes, angles, distances, and measurements in two or three dimensions. Geometry provides a mathematical foundation for structuring, interpreting, and evaluating complex datasets with hundreds or even thousands of dimensions in artificial intelligence. By treating data as points in abstract mathematical spaces, high-dimensional geometry enables intelligent systems to spot patterns, categorize items, discover connections, and make precise predictions. Gaining an understanding of these ideas enables students to see the role that geometric reasoning plays in machine learning, computer vision, natural language processing, and many other AI applications.

Points, lines, planes, circles, triangles, and solid shapes are among the common objects of traditional geometry. These ideas help explain the links between items and physical space. By extending geometry into mathematical domains that cannot be readily perceived, artificial intelligence builds on these concepts. High-dimensional spaces use numerical features that describe data properties rather than physical coordinates such as length, width, and height. A single item can be represented by hundreds or thousands of measurements at once since each feature corresponds to a single dimension. These dimensions adhere to the same mathematical rules that govern regular geometry, although they are abstract rather than physical.

In artificial intelligence, a data point is often represented as a vector of numerical values that describe its characteristics. Every value in a high-dimensional space corresponds to a coordinate. For instance, a medical diagnosis system might use measurements such as age, blood pressure, test results, and medical history to characterize a patient. In contrast, an image recognition system might use thousands of pixel intensity values to represent a photograph. Each observation becomes a point in a multidimensional geometric space, where different observations tend to appear farther apart, and comparable observations tend to appear closer together. Algorithms can effectively assess relationships between data thanks to this geometric representation.

To comprehend high-dimensional geometry, one must grasp the idea of dimensions. People are used to three spatial dimensions in daily life, yet mathematical spaces are not constrained by physical reality. While language models may use vectors with several hundred dimensions to represent words, a dataset with fifty quantifiable attributes naturally exists within a fifty-dimensional space. The mathematical space available to characterize intricate interactions grows as each new characteristic adds a coordinate. Computers use proven mathematical concepts from geometry and linear algebra to handle representations of spaces with hundreds of dimensions, even if humans are unable to see such spaces.

One of the most crucial geometric ideas in artificial intelligence is distance. A quantitative method of determining similarity is to measure the distance between two data points. In a high-dimensional space, two observations that are close to each other frequently have comparable properties. On the other hand, observations that are widely apart usually correspond to distinct categories or behaviors. Many AI applications, such as recommendation systems, picture recognition, anomaly detection, and clustering algorithms, rely on distance computations. Intelligent systems use mathematical distance measurements to find relationships that inform predictions and classifications.

Distance in high-dimensional spaces can be measured using a variety of techniques. One of the most popular is the Euclidean distance, which expands upon the well-known straight-line distance formula. Regardless of the number of dimensions involved, this measurement determines the shortest path between two places. Euclidean distance is often used by artificial intelligence to compare feature vectors that describe documents, sounds, images, and customer preferences. Determining how similar or distinct two observations are inside a mathematical space is the fundamental goal, even though other distance metrics could highlight certain traits or support specialized datasets.

Distance and similarity are closely related; similarity frequently highlights connections rather than actual isolation. Even if the magnitudes of two vectors pointing in comparable directions differ greatly, they may yet reflect closely related notions. Cosine similarity is especially useful for document analysis and natural language processing since it measures the angle of vectors rather than their absolute distance. Semantic similarity between words, sentences, or documents is often determined by comparing vector directions in search engines, recommendation systems, and language models. AI systems can identify significant links that go beyond straightforward numerical comparisons thanks to this geometric interpretation.

Another crucial element of high-dimensional geometry is the concept of coordinate systems. Each point in a mathematical space needs coordinates that indicate its position relative to selected reference axes. Coordinate systems, in which each axis represents a specific attribute or measurement, are used by artificial intelligence to represent data. Algorithms can systematically evaluate relationships while maintaining mathematical consistency when information is arranged in this manner. Additionally, coordinate representations make transformations easier by allowing data to be scaled, rotated, or projected into different spaces that are better suited for analysis.

Because they modify data representations while maintaining significant linkages, transformations are essential in high-dimensional geometry. Without losing important patterns, a transformation can compress information into fewer dimensions, rotate data, or switch coordinate systems. Transformations are often used in machine learning to increase computational efficiency, improve pattern recognition, or eliminate unnecessary complexity. By eliminating noise and unnecessary variance from datasets, mathematical transformation techniques allow intelligent systems to concentrate on significant aspects.

For artificial intelligence, dimensionality presents both opportunities and challenges. Because more features capture more specific information, higher dimensions enable richer descriptions of complicated objects. But increasing dimensionality also brings computational challenges commonly referred to as the "curse of dimensionality." Larger datasets are needed to detect significant patterns, yet distance measurements become less relevant as dimensionality increases due to the rising sparsity of data points. Knowing these difficulties enables academics to develop algorithms that perform well in extremely high-dimensional spaces.

By converting data into lower-dimensional representations while maintaining crucial information, dimensionality reduction tackles these issues. Algorithms find combinations of variables that capture the most important patterns rather than directly analyzing thousands of pieces of information. A popular mathematical method called principal component analysis spins coordinate systems to find the directions that account for the most variation in data. Large datasets can be represented using fewer dimensions without sacrificing significant structural linkages, thanks to these new directions becoming the primary components. Dimensionality reduction makes visualization and interpretation easier while increasing computing efficiency.

Because humans can only detect three spatial dimensions by nature, visualization gets more challenging as dimensionality increases. To translate high-dimensional data into two-dimensional or three-dimensional representations that may be interpreted, artificial intelligence researchers rely on mathematical projection techniques. Projections frequently show clusters, trends, and patterns that offer important insights into dataset structure, even when they cannot capture every relationship. Researchers can assess model performance, identify abnormalities, and understand correlations among observations that would otherwise go unnoticed using visualization techniques.

Another significant use of high-dimensional geometry is clustering. Clustering techniques use geometric proximity in feature space to group similar observations. By examining the distances and relationships among data points, these techniques identify natural groupings rather than relying on predefined categories. Clustering algorithms are useful for document organization, image analysis, biological categorization, and customer segmentation. Without explicit supervision, geometric reasoning enables intelligent systems to recognize salient structures within complex information.

Geometric principles also play a major role in classification algorithms. Machine learning algorithms frequently create decision boundaries between data points in high-dimensional spaces to differentiate between categories. Depending on the underlying mathematical model, these boundaries could be lines, planes, or more intricate surfaces. The side of the boundary on which new observations appear determines their classification. Neural networks, logistic regression, and support vector machines all use geometric interpretations of decision boundaries to solve classification issues.

Another example of geometry assisting AI is found in nearest neighbor techniques. By comparing neighboring samples in feature space, these algorithms categorize new data. This method is predicated on the idea that comparable objects typically fall into the same category. By identifying nearby data points via distance computations, predictions based on local geometric correlations become possible. Similar to this, recommendation algorithms recognize items or users that are close to one another in mathematical spaces, allowing for tailored recommendations based on shared traits.

Because digital images inherently contain a vast number of numerical features, computer vision heavily relies on high-dimensional geometry. Each pixel adds information about color or brightness, resulting in feature spaces with thousands or millions of dimensions. These representations are repeatedly transformed by convolutional neural networks, which extract progressively significant geometric information, including edges, textures, forms, and object components. By arranging visual data into mathematical patterns appropriate for categorization and interpretation, geometry directs recognition throughout this process.

Geometric representations of language are also essential to natural language processing. Words are transformed into high-dimensional vectors, called embeddings, by modern language models, where semantic relationships align with geometric proximity. While unrelated words stay farther apart, words with similar meanings appear near together within embedding gaps. Sentence representations allow intelligent computers to understand grammar, context, translation, and question answering by combining several word vectors through mathematical transformations. AI models can identify nuanced linguistic correlations beyond dictionary definitions thanks to geometric reasoning.

During learning, geometric representations are constantly reshaped by neural networks. While later computing layers convert raw input data into increasingly abstract mathematical spaces that highlight patterns pertinent to particular tasks, early computational layers handle raw input features. Every modification alters the geometric relationships among data points, making it easier to distinguish between categories and bringing similar observations closer together. This gradual improvement shows how geometry facilitates learning by arranging data into representations that enable precise classification and prediction.

Another field in which high-dimensional geometry is crucial is optimization. Navigating intricate mathematical environments defined by objective functions is a necessary part of training machine learning models. A point in an incredibly high-dimensional optimization space corresponds to every possible combination of model parameters. Gradient-based optimization techniques gradually improve model performance by moving systematically across these mathematical surfaces along directions that reduce prediction error. It is easier to understand how intelligent systems effectively learn from data when optimization is understood geometrically.

Real-world applications show how useful high-dimensional geometry is. To aid in diagnosis and treatment planning, healthcare systems examine patient data that is represented in multidimensional spaces. Financial institutions use observations that deviate from typical behavioral clusters to identify fraudulent transactions. Geometric models that describe their surroundings are used by autonomous cars to interpret sensor data. Scientists use high-dimensional representations to arrange genetic data, revealing biological linkages that are not readily observable. Geometric reasoning converts complicated numerical data into insightful information that facilitates wise decision-making in a variety of situations.

Broader analytical thinking is also strengthened by studying geometry in high-dimensional data representation. As they understand the relationship between conventional geometry and contemporary computational science, learners gain intuition about spatial relationships, pattern identification, abstraction, and mathematical modeling. Students see geometry as a universal language that describes relationships within complicated information rather than just the study of physical shapes. This broader perspective provides valuable preparation for more complex subjects such as robotics, artificial intelligence, data science, and machine learning.

In the end, one of the most potent mathematical frameworks supporting intelligent systems is provided by geometry in high-dimensional data representation.

Artificial intelligence can organize data, evaluate similarity, find patterns, categorize observations, and improve prediction models by extending well-known geometric concepts into abstract multidimensional spaces. Together, ideas like vectors, distances, transformations, coordinate systems, grouping, and decision boundaries build mathematical environments that facilitate learning. High-dimensional geometry will continue to be a crucial basis for understanding how machines evaluate data and make informed judgments as artificial intelligence spreads across healthcare, finance, education, engineering, research, and innumerable other domains. Gaining a solid grasp of these geometric ideas gives students the mathematical expertise needed to investigate cutting-edge AI technologies and contribute to upcoming advancements powered by computer, data, and mathematical reasoning.

Applications of Linear Algebra in Machine Learning Models

One of the most fundamental areas of mathematics underpinning contemporary artificial intelligence and machine learning is linear algebra. The mathematical basis that enables these technologies to operate effectively is largely rooted in linear algebra, even though many people associate artificial intelligence with complex algorithms and powerful computing systems. Concepts such as vectors, matrices, linear transformations, and matrix operations are essential at every step of a machine learning model, from data representation and computation to prediction optimization and accuracy enhancement. These mathematical techniques enable computers to perform intricate computations quickly, organize vast volumes of data, and uncover significant patterns hidden in data. Learners gain important insight into how intelligent systems absorb information and make accurate predictions by understanding the role of linear algebra in machine learning models.

Instead of depending solely on human-written instructions, computers can learn patterns from data through a process called machine learning. Machine learning algorithms evaluate samples and find mathematical patterns that enable them to make predictions about new data rather than developing a different rule for every scenario. The language and computational framework needed for this learning process are provided by linear algebra. Since vectors and matrices are used to represent data, model parameters, predictions, and intermediate computations, linear algebra is a crucial part of almost all machine learning methods. It would be computationally impossible to process the massive datasets needed by contemporary artificial intelligence without these mathematical structures.

Data representation is one of the first uses of linear algebra in machine learning. Information gathered from observations, experiments, sensors, documents, or user interactions is the starting point for every machine learning model. Before processing, this data is arranged in numerical form. In a matrix, each observation is represented by a row, and a distinct column represents each feature or characteristic. For instance, features like location, size, age, number of bedrooms, and neighborhood characteristics may be included in a dataset that predicts home prices. Instead of examining each record individually, computers can examine all observations at once when the dataset is represented as a matrix. Model construction is simplified, and this well-organized mathematical structure significantly improves computational performance.

Because they represent individual observations, model parameters, predictions, and feature values, vectors are also crucial to machine learning. Vectors with multiple numerical measurements can represent a single image, document, medical record, or customer profile. Vectors are used to hold word embeddings in natural language processing, pixel values in computer vision, and sensor readings in robotics. Algorithms can compare data, quantify similarities, and carry out computations using standardized operations thanks to their mathematical representations. Machine learning systems may process a wide variety of data using a common mathematical framework due to the flexibility of vectors.

One of the most common processes in machine learning is matrix multiplication. This process allows models to efficiently transform data by combining information from multiple matrices subject to precisely defined mathematical constraints. Many sophisticated AI systems are powered by neural networks, which rely heavily on repeated matrix multiplication. A neural network's layers create new representations that capture ever-more complicated patterns by multiplying input vectors by weight matrices. As models learn from data, millions or even billions of matrix multiplications may take place during training. Therefore, one of the main reasons specialized hardware, such as graphics processing units, performs remarkably well in machine learning tasks is the efficient execution of this procedure.

One of the most basic applications of linear algebra in machine learning is linear regression. By finding mathematical connections between input variables and target values, linear regression forecasts numerical results. Using coefficient vectors that explain how each feature contributes to the final prediction, the model illustrates these linkages. By simultaneously solving systems of linear equations for all training cases, matrix operations enable efficient estimation of these coefficients. Despite being theoretically simple, linear regression illustrates many of the fundamental mathematical concepts used in more sophisticated machine learning techniques.

Similar concepts are extended by logistic regression to classification problems, where predictions are made using categories rather than numerical values. Logistic regression determines the likelihood that observations fall into specific classifications rather than estimating continuous quantities. During model training, matrix operations efficiently calculate and arrange feature information. Until classification accuracy increases, optimization algorithms make periodic adjustments to parameter vectors. Both linear and logistic regression rely heavily on linear algebra to represent data and perform computations effectively, despite their different goals.

Perhaps the most significant use of linear algebra in contemporary artificial intelligence is found in neural networks. Each artificial neuron receives vectorized numerical inputs, multiplies them by weight matrices, adds bias values, and produces modified outputs. These outputs serve as inputs to later layers, resulting in a series of matrix operations that progressively transform unprocessed data into insightful forecasts. Neural networks are used in many different fields, including generative AI, audio processing, image identification, and language translation. It would be impossible to build and train these complex models without linear algebra.

Because weight matrices contain the modifiable parameters learned during neural network training, they warrant special consideration. These matrices initially have numerical values that are assigned at random. Optimization techniques adjust individual components during training to reduce prediction errors. Based on mathematical correlations between inputs, outputs, and detected mistakes, each update is a meticulously computed modification. Therefore, weight matrices are essential components of intelligent systems that can adapt through experience, as they represent the knowledge gained through learning.

Another significant use of linear algebra is featuring transformation. Raw datasets frequently contain data that is challenging for algorithms to interpret immediately. Through mathematical transformations, original features are transformed into alternative representations that highlight significant patterns while eliminating superfluous complexity. These alterations are naturally performed via matrix multiplication, which generates new feature spaces in which learning is more efficient. Neural networks increasingly extract higher-level features important for prediction by continually transforming data internally. Feature transformation shows how linear algebra improves model correctness and processing efficiency.

A popular method for reducing dimensionality that relies solely on linear algebra is principal component analysis. Numerous datasets have hundreds or thousands of features, which raises the possibility of overfitting and makes computation costly. Principal component analysis reduces variable redundancy by identifying data paths that capture the most variance. The most instructive features of the dataset are represented by these directions, which constitute new coordinate axes. Machine learning models function more effectively without sacrificing crucial information by projecting observations onto fewer dimensions. This method demonstrates how linear algebra preserves meaningful relationships while simplifying complex datasets.

Another potent linear algebraic method that is often used in machine learning is singular value decomposition. By breaking down matrices into more manageable parts, this mathematical process uncovers hidden patterns in data. Singular value decomposition is useful for latent semantic analysis, recommendation systems, image compression, and natural language processing because it finds underlying patterns that are hard to see directly. Algorithms can handle data more effectively and improve interpretability by breaking down large matrices into smaller mathematical components.

Another area where linear algebra plays a major role is similarity measurement. Comparing observations to assess how similar they are is necessary for many machine learning applications. These interactions are quantified scientifically using vector operations like cosine similarity and dot products. Search engines assess the importance of documents, recommendation systems compare consumer preference vectors, and language models use these computations to find semantic similarities between words. Accurate similarity measurement allows intelligent systems to find pertinent content, organize data, and provide tailored recommendations.

Because digital images are inherently matrices of pixel values, computer vision strongly relies on linear algebra. Numerical data representing brightness and color intensity over thousands or millions of pixels can be found in every photograph. Convolutional neural networks use additional matrices to represent mathematical filters for examining these filters. Edges, textures, forms, and progressively more intricate visual elements are identified through successive matrix operations. Medical imaging, autonomous driving, facial recognition, and object recognition all rely on linear algebra for effective image analysis.

Another interesting application is natural language processing. In contemporary language models, words are represented as vectors called embeddings, where geometric relationships capture semantic content. Algorithms can comprehend context and relationships between concepts because similar phrases occupy neighboring positions in high-dimensional vector spaces. Language models can analyze grammar, respond to queries, summarize materials, and translate between languages because matrix transformations continuously update their embeddings as they process sentences. Thus, many modern language technologies are mathematically based on linear algebra.

Another crucial use of linear algebra in machine learning is optimization methods. To enhance predictive performance, models continuously update parameter vectors and matrices throughout training. One of the most popular optimization techniques, gradient descent, determines which directions minimize prediction errors. Numerous vector and matrix operations are used in each training cycle to update model parameters methodically. Efficient linear algebra computations are necessary for large-scale AI systems with billions of trainable parameters to complete training in a reasonable amount of time.

Another machine learning method with a strong linear algebraic foundation is support vector machines. By identifying mathematical boundaries that separate several categories in high-dimensional spaces, these algorithms classify observations. While matrix computations find the best decision boundaries that maximize classification accuracy, vector operations identify commonalities between observations. Support vector machines show how geometric interpretations of linear algebra facilitate efficient pattern recognition in a variety of applications, including financial analysis, medical diagnosis, and handwriting detection.

Additionally, recommendation systems rely heavily on linear algebra. Social media sites, streaming platforms, and online retailers use big matrices that show preferences and behaviors to study user-product interactions. By identifying hidden links in these interactions, matrix factorization techniques allow systems to suggest information that is likely to be of interest to specific users. These techniques, which offer highly customized experiences backed solely by mathematical analysis, have revolutionized internet commerce and entertainment.

The widespread use of linear algebra in machine learning is further evident in scientific computing and engineering. Molecular biology, robotics, astronomy, healthcare, economics, and climate modeling all produce massive datasets that need to be efficiently processed mathematically. Machine learning algorithms use vectors, matrices, and transformations to gain significant insights from these datasets. Linear algebra offers the computational framework that allows intelligent algorithms to function well, whether they are used to analyze satellite imagery, control robotic systems, or anticipate the course of diseases.

One of the biggest benefits of linear algebra is still its computational efficiency. To execute vector and matrix operations quickly using parallel computation, modern processors and graphics processing units have been specifically designed. These hardware devices significantly speed up machine learning training and prediction by performing numerous operations concurrently rather than processing computations sequentially. Therefore, as artificial intelligence models continue to grow in size and complexity, advances in specialized technology have strengthened the significance of linear algebra.

Additionally, understanding linear algebra fosters important analytical abilities that go beyond machine learning. As they develop an understanding of the mathematical ideas behind intelligent technology, learners improve their logical reasoning, pattern recognition, abstraction, and methodical problem-solving skills. Instead of seeing computational models as enigmatic black boxes, students who comprehend vectors, matrices, transformations, and matrix operations can more confidently interpret complex AI concepts.

In the end, the use of linear algebra in machine learning models shows that the real force behind contemporary artificial intelligence is mathematics. Vectors, matrices, and linear transformations must collaborate well at every stage of learning, from organizing datasets and translating features to optimizing parameters and producing predictions. The computational power and mathematical accuracy of linear algebra are essential for neural networks, recommendation systems, computer vision, natural language processing, optimization, and dimensionality reduction. Linear algebra will continue to be a crucial foundation for creativity and sound decision-making as machine learning advances across a variety of fields, including healthcare, finance, education, transportation, scientific research, and many more. By grasping these mathematical ideas, students get the information needed to comprehend current AI technologies as well as the abilities needed to contribute to the creation of increasingly complex intelligent systems in the future.

CHAPTER III
Calculus, Optimization, and Learning Algorithms

Limits, Derivatives, and Rates of Change

Calculus's foundational ideas of limits, derivatives, and rates of change are essential to mathematics, science, engineering, and artificial intelligence. These subjects illustrate how numbers and systems change over time, and how complex problems can be optimized, despite being frequently presented as theoretical mathematical concepts. Calculus offers the mathematical foundation for algorithms in artificial intelligence and machine learning to enhance their performance by modifying internal parameters in response to observable errors. Neural networks rely on concepts closely linked to limits, derivatives, and rates of change every time they learn from data, identify patterns more precisely, or improve their predictions. Gaining an understanding of these ideas enables students to see how mathematical reasoning converts static formulas into dynamic systems that can adapt and learn continuously.

Calculus is one of the most important areas of mathematics because it was developed to study continuous change. Calculus examines how values change across different contexts, in contrast to arithmetic and algebra, which often focus on fixed quantities and relationships. Instead of being discrete occurrences, many technological and natural processes involve constant change. People develop over time, cars accelerate and decelerate, temperatures vary during the day, and financial markets are always changing. As mathematical parameters are adjusted often to enhance predicted performance, artificial intelligence models similarly undergo constant change throughout training. Calculus provides the tools to examine and understand these dynamic systems.

Calculus is based on the idea of a limit. The value that a mathematical expression approaches when its input approaches a specific point is described by a limit. Limits look at behavior near particular conditions rather than at precise numbers. This concept enables mathematicians to investigate scenarios in which direct assessment might be challenging or unfeasible. Limits offer a thorough way to define derivatives, analyze continuity, and comprehend how functions react in changing conditions. Limits play a role in the mathematical theory that underpins optimization algorithms and numerical techniques used in model training in artificial intelligence.

Imagine approaching a goal without necessarily arriving there right away. This is a natural method of understanding constraints. The associated output gets closer to a predicted outcome as the input gets closer to a specific value. Mathematicians can study gradual transitions instead of sudden shifts because of this idea. Repeated approximations that gradually approach desired solutions are the foundation of many computational algorithms. Thus, being aware of limitations enables students to see that many AI techniques advance through gradual improvement rather than instantaneous perfection.

Because a continuous function changes smoothly without abrupt jumps or breaks, continuity and limits are intimately related. Because they enable optimization algorithms to change parameters progressively and predictably, continuous mathematical models are very useful in machine learning. Small parameter changes could lead to surprising shifts in model behavior if functions have many discontinuities, making learning challenging. For machine learning processes to be stable and effective, designing continuous objective functions is crucial.

One of the most potent concepts in mathematics is the derivative, which naturally arises from the concept of limits. The rate at which a function changes in relation to one of its variables is measured by a derivative. It expresses the instantaneous rate of change at a specific point in time. Derivatives show exactly how quantities change over time, whereas average rates of change look at behavior over time. Derivatives are essential for evaluating dynamic systems, such as physical motion, economic trends, and artificial intelligence optimization, due to their analytical power.

Motion is one of the most well-known applications of derivatives. A car's position varies over time as it moves along a road. Velocity is represented by the derivative of position with respect to time, whereas the derivative of velocity represents acceleration. These connections show how derivatives characterize ongoing change in physical systems. Similar logic is used by artificial intelligence to examine changing mathematical models. Derivatives assess how prediction errors alter as model parameters are changed rather than quantifying actual movement. Learning algorithms are guided toward increasingly precise solutions by this information.

Another geometric way to understand derivatives is to look at a curve's slope. The derivative is the slope of the tangent line that touches the curve at each point along a smooth curve. Values rise when the derivative is positive and fall when it is negative. Points where functions reach local maximum or minimum values are frequently indicated with a derivative equal to zero. These geometric interpretations are crucial to machine learning optimization because training algorithms look for parameter values that minimize prediction errors. Thus, an understanding of slopes helps explain how intelligent systems learn from data while navigating mathematical environments.

By explaining how one quantity reacts to changes in another, rates of change increase the usefulness of derivatives. Rates of change are involved in many real-world occurrences. Birth and death rates determine population growth; chemical reactions occur at different rates; stock prices change with market conditions; and biological systems change over time. Derivatives quantify how prediction accuracy reacts to parameter changes, and artificial intelligence models undergo comparable changes as learning advances. Researchers can better comprehend system behavior and forecast future results by analyzing rates of change.

Because machine learning models often incorporate multiple variables simultaneously, partial derivatives are particularly important in artificial intelligence. A partial derivative quantifies how a function changes when only one variable change while others stay constant, whereas an ordinary derivative looks at changes with respect to one variable. Millions or even billions of tunable parameters can be found in neural networks, and each one affects model performance uniquely. Partial derivatives are crucial for large-scale machine learning because they enable optimization algorithms to ascertain how altering specific parameters impacts prediction accuracy.

Gradient vectors describe the direction of greatest rise within a function by combining several partial derivatives into a single mathematical object. Gradients in optimization offer important insights into how objective functions react to changes in parameters. Machine learning algorithms use gradient information to improve performance rather than randomly exploring possibilities. While lowering computational effort, this mathematical guidance significantly improves learning efficiency. Thus, one of the most useful applications of derivatives in artificial intelligence is the gradient vector.

One of the most used optimization methods in machine learning, gradient descent, shows how derivatives can be applied directly. Gradient descent repeatedly modifies model parameters in directions that oppose the gradient to decrease prediction errors. Moving in the opposite direction minimizes mistakes since gradients show the direction of greatest increase. Derivatives are computed, parameters are updated, and improvement is assessed with each training round. Machine learning models gradually improve in accuracy through thousands or millions of these small tweaks. The mathematical concepts of derivatives and rates of change are essential to this learning process.

Another key idea closely related to optimization is the learning rate. The learning rate determines the size of parameter changes performed at each optimization stage. Models may overshoot ideal solutions and become unstable if changes are made excessively. Learning proceeds very slowly if changes are made too little. Thus, choosing the right learning rates strikes a balance between stability and efficiency. This idea shows how knowledge of rates of change extends beyond mathematical theory to real-world choices that impact the performance of artificial intelligence.

Another crucial mathematics tool for neural network training is the chain rule. Multiple interconnected layers of computation make up neural networks, each transforming data before passing it on. Applying the chain rule to derivatives across successive transformations determines how modifications in prior layers affect final predictions. Across this mathematical process, incorrect information can be distributed backward across the network via optimization algorithms, allowing each parameter to receive the necessary changes. It would be computationally impossible to train deep neural networks without the chain rule.

One of the most significant uses of derivatives in contemporary artificial intelligence is backpropagation. Neural networks process incoming data through several layers to produce initial predictions during training. Next, by comparing outputs with known target values, prediction errors are quantified. The chain rule is used in backpropagation to compute derivatives that show how each parameter affects the total error. Optimization algorithms use these derivatives to adjust weights systematically, thereby enhancing model performance. This mathematical procedure is the foundation of all successful deep learning applications, from language production to picture recognition.

Loss functions further illustrate the significance of calculus in machine learning. The degree to which model predictions and actual observations agree is measured by a loss function. Reducing this loss as much as possible is the goal of training. Derivatives give optimization algorithms direction by describing how the loss varies with respect to changes in parameters. All machine learning tasks rely on derivatives for efficient learning, but they require various loss functions. Thus, calculus establishes a direct link between mathematical modeling and the creation of useful algorithms.

Neural networks are not the only applications. Derivatives are used in linear regression to find parameter values that minimize prediction errors. Gradient-guided optimization techniques are the foundation of logistic regression. Calculus is used during training in support vector machines, probabilistic models, reinforcement learning algorithms, and many other machine learning approaches. Derivatives provide mathematical information that enables systematic improvement through repeated parameter tweaks, regardless of the specific algorithm.

Another interesting example is computer vision. By optimizing millions of numerical parameters based on visual data, image recognition algorithms can identify things. By determining how changes in these parameters affect classification accuracy, derivatives enable optimization algorithms to improve performance gradually. Autonomous vehicles, medical imaging technologies, speech recognition, and handwriting analysis all follow similar principles. Rates of change direct intelligent systems toward more precise interpretations of complex data in each application.

Calculus is also necessary for natural language processing. Language models understand relationships between words, sentences, and circumstances to produce meaningful replies. Derivatives evaluate how parameter changes affect prediction quality during training, allowing optimization algorithms to improve language comprehension continuously. Derivatives and gradient-based optimization are essential to the remarkable performance of contemporary conversational AI, translation systems, summarization tools, and question-answering applications.

Limits, derivatives, and rates of change are also very helpful in scientific inquiry. Biologists model population dynamics, engineers optimize structural designs, economists explore market fluctuations, physicists use differential equations to describe motion, and climate scientists examine shifting climatic conditions. By fusing machine learning with calculus-based mathematical models, artificial intelligence is increasingly enhancing these domains. This interdisciplinary cooperation demonstrates the ongoing significance of derivatives in scientific research and technological advancement.

Beyond its immediate uses, learning calculus fosters more general analytical thinking. Students gain a stronger comprehension of mathematical modeling, logical reasoning, continuous processes, and problem-solving techniques. Instead of seeing mathematics as discrete formulas, students see how abstract ideas accurately explain real-world situations. When tackling increasingly complex scientific and computational problems, this viewpoint promotes curiosity, intellectual adaptability, and confidence.

Because limits and derivatives present new perspectives on change, many students initially find them difficult. Nonetheless, natural links between mathematical definitions and real-world applications are progressively revealed via regular practice. Conceptual comprehension is strengthened by solving practical issues, analyzing graphs, visualizing function behavior, and investigating computational instances. As students get comfortable with these concepts, they find that calculus offers sophisticated answers to issues that were previously thought to be too complicated for methodical examination.

In the end, limits, derivatives, and rates of change provide the mathematical framework that enables intelligent systems to continuously learn, adapt, and improve. Derivatives quantify instantaneous change, limits provide precise definitions that characterize behavior near crucial points, and rates of change link mathematical theory to dynamic real-world systems. These ideas operate together to support prediction models, neural network training, optimization algorithms, and a plethora of other applications of artificial intelligence. Calculus continues to be a vital tool for understanding dynamic systems and developing technology that learns from experience across a variety of fields, including healthcare, engineering, finance, robotics, and natural language processing. By grasping these fundamental ideas, students gain a crucial understanding of the mathematical elegance of calculus and its revolutionary contributions to contemporary artificial intelligence, science, and technology.

Gradient Descent and Optimization Techniques

Among the most crucial mathematical ideas in machine learning and artificial intelligence are gradient descent and optimization strategies. Instead of relying solely on preset instructions, they provide processes that enable intelligent systems to learn from data and improve their performance. Every effective machine learning model must undergo a learning process that modifies its internal mathematical parameters, regardless of whether it is used to detect images, translate languages, forecast financial trends, or produce text that resembles human writing. Because gradient descent progressively reduces prediction errors through iterative updates, it is one of the most popular optimization techniques for achieving this objective. Learners may realize how artificial intelligence evolves from basic mathematical models to highly accurate systems that can solve challenging real-world problems by understanding gradient descent and optimization techniques.

The mathematical technique of identifying the optimum option from numerous options is known as optimization. Optimization happens in daily life when people look for the quickest way to get somewhere, the best use of resources, or the best return on investment. By determining the parameter values that yield the most accurate predictions, optimization in artificial intelligence aims to enhance machine learning models. Optimization algorithms adhere to meticulously crafted mathematical processes that direct learning toward progressively more efficient solutions rather than haphazardly exploring an infinite number of options. Even when working with massive datasets and millions of configurable factors, intelligent systems can still improve thanks to this methodical approach.

The initial parameters of machine learning models are often set to arbitrary numerical values. These parameters control how the model interprets data and makes predictions. Early projections are typically unreliable since the initial values are selected without prior information. The goal of training is to adjust these parameters until the model gradually produces reliable results. The mathematical foundation for implementing these modifications in a rational and structured way is provided by optimization techniques. Optimization algorithms assess prediction errors and decide how each parameter should be adjusted to improve performance, rather than adjusting parameters at random.

The idea of a loss function is essential to this learning process. A loss function quantifies the discrepancy between the results observed in the training data and the predictions produced by a machine learning model. The loss value stays low if forecasts closely resemble the anticipated outcomes. The loss increases if forecasts diverge considerably. Because reduced loss typically translates into improved prediction accuracy, the main objective of optimization is to minimize it. While different machine learning tasks call for different loss functions, they all aim to provide a numerical representation of the model's performance.

The most popular optimization technique for minimizing loss functions is gradient descent. Two key concepts are reflected in its name. While "descent" denotes movement in the opposite direction toward smaller values, "gradient" refers to the mathematical quantity that describes the direction and rate of the greatest increase in a function. Gradient descent repeatedly advances in the opposite direction of the gradient since optimization aims to decrease the loss rather than increase it. The method progressively approaches a point where prediction errors become negligible by taking several small downhill steps on the mathematical landscape defined by the loss function.

Imagining yourself standing on a mountain shrouded in thick fog is a helpful method to understand gradient decline. It is impossible to see the whole terrain at once due to limited visibility. Nonetheless, it is possible to descend toward the valley below by noting the steepest downward slope at each step. Moving downward frequently eventually leads to a lower elevation, even if each step is tiny. A similar approach is used in machine learning. The method can best identify the path that minimizes loss, but it cannot immediately find the optimal parameter values. It progressively approaches an ideal answer through numerous upgrades.

Derivatives are used to compute the gradient. Derivatives quantify the rate at which the loss varies with each parameter. A parameter's derivative becomes comparatively large when it has a significant impact on prediction accuracy. The related derivative stays modest when changing a parameter has minimal impact. Together, these derivatives form a gradient vector that indicates how each modifiable parameter affects the loss function. Instead of relying on speculation or haphazard experimentation, gradient descent can adjust parameters intelligently thanks to this mathematical understanding.

Another crucial element of gradient descent is the learning rate. The learning rate determines the magnitude of each optimization adjustment. The algorithm may overshoot the ideal solution if the learning rate is very high, which could result in unstable behavior or completely block convergence. On the other hand, learning proceeds very slowly if the learning rate is too low since parameter changes become nearly meaningless. Stability and speed must be balanced when choosing an optimal learning rate. To increase efficiency and dependability, many real-world machine learning systems use adaptive techniques that automatically modify learning rates throughout training.

The machine learning model is first fed training data to start the optimization process. The model makes predictions using its current parameters and compares them to known goal values. Derivatives show how each parameter contributed to the prediction error, which is calculated using the loss function. To minimize errors in the future, gradient descent modifies each parameter slightly in the direction of the gradient. Until the model performs satisfactorily or meets predetermined stopping criteria, this cycle is repeated over a large number of training samples. Intelligent systems can learn from experience in a mathematically valid way by repeatedly using this process.

Batch gradient descent is one of the earliest types of gradient descent. In this method, before updating any parameters, the algorithm computes gradients using the complete training dataset. The resulting gradients are steady and dependable because every available example is used in the computation. However, processing each observation before each update takes a significant amount of time and computer resources when datasets are very large. Millions of training samples are often used in modern machine learning applications, making batch-based approaches less useful for many real-world problems.

An alternate approach that modifies parameters after processing a single training example at a time is stochastic gradient descent. The algorithm makes regular modifications based on individual observations rather than waiting to evaluate the entire dataset. These changes happen far more quickly, enabling quicker training development. Repeated updates typically increase the model's performance, even if individual parameter changes may vary due to its reliance on incomplete data. The computational efficiency of stochastic gradient descent has made it particularly useful for training large-scale machine learning models.

By processing small groups of training samples at each update, mini-batch gradient descent combines the advantages of both earlier approaches. The approach computes gradients from manageable subsets, known as mini-batches, rather than using the entire dataset or a single observation. This method strikes a balance between consistent learning behavior and computational efficiency. Additionally, mini-batch techniques leverage modern hardware that can efficiently perform simultaneous matrix computations. As a result, they are now the recommended optimization method for training deep neural networks across numerous AI applications.

Seldom are optimization landscapes straightforward. Several machine learning problems have complicated surfaces with several hills, valleys, and flat areas, rather than a single smooth valley that leads directly to the ideal answer. Although there may be better answers elsewhere, local minima are places where all surrounding directions seem higher. Saddle points pose additional difficulties because, even in the absence of ideal solutions, gradients become extremely small. Gradient descent must negotiate these challenging mathematical environments while avoiding roadblocks that could impede learning or lower the accuracy of the final model.

Momentum is an optimization method that uses data from prior parameter modifications to enhance gradient descent. Momentum maintains steady progress toward optimal solutions by accumulating previous movements rather than just the current gradient. This strategy is similar to pushing a big thing downhill. After gaining speed, the item keeps going even when it comes across minor obstacles in its route. Similarly, momentum accelerates convergence toward better solutions while helping optimization algorithms overcome oscillations and shallow local minima.

These concepts are expanded upon by adaptive optimization techniques, which automatically modify learning rates for certain parameters. Throughout training, algorithms like AdaGrad, RMSProp, and Adam keep an eye on prior gradient data to calculate the proper update sizes. Smaller updates may be applied to parameters that change quickly, while greater adjustments may be made to those that change more slowly. Particularly for deep neural networks with millions of parameters and diverse learning properties, these adaptive approaches often improve training efficiency. Adaptive optimization has therefore gained widespread use in numerous machine learning applications.

One of the best ways to see gradient descent in action is through neural networks. Each artificial neuron takes numerical inputs, multiplies them by adjustable weights, sums the results, and generates outputs that are sent to the layers below. At first, bad forecasts are produced by randomly assigned weights. Backpropagation computes gradients that explain how each weight affects prediction errors during training. The weights are then updated using gradient descent. Neural networks can detect images, understand language, generate text, and perform numerous other intelligent tasks with incredible accuracy by repeating this process thousands or millions of times.

Because backpropagation provides a mathematical mechanism for computing gradients in multilayer neural networks, it is closely related to gradient descent. Backpropagation uses the chain rule to propagate error information backward through successive layers rather than computing derivatives for each parameter separately. It is feasible to train incredibly large neural networks with millions or billions of configurable parameters thanks to this efficient processing. Modern deep learning would not be computationally possible without the cooperation of gradient descent and backpropagation.

Additionally, optimization strategies are crucial for enhancing generality and avoiding overfitting. Because it has remembered specifics rather than learned meaningful patterns, a model that matches training data flawlessly may perform poorly when faced with new information. More mathematical restrictions are introduced via regularization techniques, which promote easier, more universal solutions. By enhancing the model's performance on previously unseen data, weight decay, dropout, and early halting all support gradient-based optimization. These methods show that effective optimization requires not only reducing training error but also striking a balance between resilience and precision.

Gradient descent has several uses in artificial intelligence. Computer vision systems use optimization to enhance object detection and image classification. Natural language processing models use gradient descent to acquire vocabulary, grammar, and contextual relationships. While recommendation systems fine-tune predictions based on user preferences, speech recognition systems optimize parameters to distinguish spoken words accurately. Financial systems enhance fraud detection, healthcare applications boost diagnostic models, and autonomous cars continuously improve decision-making. Instead of remaining fixed after initial programming, optimization enables intelligent systems to adapt through experience across a variety of sectors.

Another crucial factor in optimization is computational efficiency. During training, modern machine learning models may have billions of parameters, necessitating innumerable mathematical changes. By executing numerous matrix operations simultaneously, graphics processing units and specialized hardware accelerate these computations. The advantages of this hardware are maximized by effective optimization techniques, which cut the training time from months to days or even hours. Therefore, ongoing optimization advances support both the practical implementation of increasingly complex artificial intelligence systems and greater model accuracy.

Studying optimization methods like gradient descent also improves general mathematical comprehension. Students gain a deeper understanding of calculus, linear algebra, numerical analysis, and computational thinking, as well as how various fields collaborate to address real-world issues. Optimization serves as an example of how mathematical theory is not limited to textbooks but rather actively propels technological advancements that impact scientific research, healthcare, education, communication, transportation, and finance.

In the end, the mathematical engine that enables machine learning models to improve through experience continuously is provided by gradient-based optimization methods. Intelligent systems convert raw data into precise predictions and significant decisions by systematically minimizing loss functions, computing gradients via derivatives, and updating parameters with well-designed algorithms. Batch methods, stochastic approaches, mini-batch tactics, momentum, adaptive learning techniques, and regularization facilitate more effective and dependable learning. Optimization will continue to be one of the most important mathematical underpinnings of artificial intelligence as it continues to permeate every facet of contemporary civilization. A solid grasp of gradient descent gives students important insight into how intelligent systems learn, adapt, and change. This knowledge is essential for investigating cutting-edge machine learning techniques and contributing to upcoming advancements in computational science and artificial intelligence.

Partial Derivatives and Multivariable Calculus

Multivariable calculus and partial derivatives are fundamental mathematical concepts that underpin many contemporary scientific and technological domains, including machine learning and artificial intelligence. Many real-world issues involve multiple variables interacting simultaneously, whereas elementary calculus focuses on functions of a single variable. Artificial intelligence systems analyze large volumes of data, and forecasts are impacted by hundreds, thousands, or even millions of interrelated variables. While partial derivatives enable researchers and engineers to understand how individual variables contribute to overall system behavior, multivariable calculus provides the mathematical tools to examine these intricate interactions. By grasping these ideas, students may better understand how intelligent systems learn from data, improve through optimization, and solve challenging problems across a variety of applications.

Although calculus was originally developed to study motion and continuous change, its concepts readily apply to systems with many variables. Few circumstances in daily life rely solely on one element. Temperature, humidity, air pressure, and wind speed all affect the weather. Employment, output, investment, and consumer demand all contribute to economic growth. Age, symptoms, test results, genetic information, and lifestyle choices are all taken into account when making medical diagnoses. Similarly, artificial intelligence examines datasets using a variety of factors that together affect predictions. The mathematical foundation required to comprehend and effectively simulate these interrelated relationships is provided by multivariable calculus.

An output value is assigned by a function of many variables based on more than one input. For instance, a multivariable function may depend on temperature, pressure, and volume all at once rather than expressing a quantity only as a function of time. Because machine learning models make predictions based on combinations of numerous features, they operate similarly. Location, floor area, age, neighborhood quality, transit accessibility, and market circumstances may all be taken into account concurrently in a model that forecasts home values. Functions that capture interactions among several variables, rather than individual influences, are needed to represent these relationships formally.

Because human intuition is inherently restricted to three-dimensional space, visualizing multivariable functions can initially appear difficult. Functions of one variable produce curves, but functions of two variables frequently produce surfaces. Direct visualization is not feasible when there are more than three variables. Nevertheless, dimensionality has no bearing on the mathematical ideas. Artificial intelligence often operates in environments with hundreds or thousands of dimensions, each representing a distinct dataset attribute. Multivariable calculus provides rigorous mathematical techniques for understanding these high-dimensional spaces, even though they cannot be directly examined.

One of the most crucial techniques in multivariable calculus is the partial derivative. When all other variables are held constant, a partial derivative calculates how a function changes in relation to one particular variable. This sets partial derivatives apart from regular derivatives, which are defined only for functions of a single independent variable. Partial derivatives enable researchers to determine how each distinct feature affects the behavior of a complex mathematical system by isolating the effect of one variable at a time. This skill is crucial to artificial intelligence, as machine learning models often include many modifiable parameters that must be examined individually during optimization.

Imagine a landscape with hills and valleys to gain an intuitive understanding of partial derivatives. Both horizontal coordinates determine each point's elevation. The rate of elevation change indicates one partial derivative if a person goes just east or west while staying in the same north-south position. The rate of change that results from walking solely north or south while maintaining a constant east-west position is another partial derivative. When taken as a whole, these measures show how the terrain shifts in various directions. Because prediction errors vary with the parameter being changed, machine learning models exhibit similar behavior.

The particular function of partial derivatives is reflected in their notation. Mathematicians use a modified notation that indicates differentiation with respect to one selected variable while treating all other variables as constants, rather than the standard derivative symbol. The basic principle behind the notation is simple, even though it may seem strange at first. Partial derivatives make it easier to analyze extremely complicated systems in which numerous factors interact simultaneously by considering one variable at a time. Even in situations when direct observation is not feasible, this methodical approach allows for effective mathematical reasoning.

The flexibility of partial derivatives to show varying sensitivity is one of its biggest advantages. While some factors have very small effects, others have a substantial impact on results. By calculating how the output changes as individual inputs vary, partial derivatives provide a mathematical way to quantify these changes. Understanding sensitivity is important in artificial intelligence because optimization algorithms use this knowledge to determine which parameters should remain relatively stable and which require larger adjustments. As a result, partial derivatives prevent needless computational effort while directing machine learning toward more precise predictions.

Another crucial concept closely associated with partial derivatives is the gradient vector. All of a multivariable function's partial derivatives are combined into a single vector to create a gradient. This vector shows how quickly the function changes in that direction and points toward the direction of the function's greatest increase. Gradients are mathematical guides that steer algorithms toward better solutions in optimization issues. Gradient vectors are often used in machine learning models during training because they show how each modifiable parameter affects prediction errors.

Gradients built from partial derivatives are the sole basis for gradient descent, one of the most popular optimization methods in artificial intelligence. A loss function is used to quantify prediction errors during model training. The gradient integrates this data into a single mathematical direction, whereas partial derivatives determine how altering each parameter affects the loss. To minimize prediction errors, the optimization algorithm then advances in the direction opposite to the gradient. By using multivariable calculus to provide direction, machine learning models progressively improve their performance over thousands or millions of repeated updates.

Perhaps the most significant use of partial derivatives in contemporary artificial intelligence is found in neural networks. Millions, or perhaps billions, of customizable weights and biases are present in the many interconnected layers that make up these networks. All of these factors must cooperate for the network to produce any forecast. Partial derivatives are used to determine how each unique weight affects the final prediction error during training. Using this data, optimization algorithms can gradually improve overall accuracy by adjusting each parameter. It would be computationally unfeasible to train huge neural networks without partial derivatives.

Another amazing use of multivariable calculus is backpropagation. Backpropagation effectively uses the chain rule to convey error information backward through all network layers rather than computing derivatives separately for each parameter. Partial derivatives describe relationships between adjacent layers, and each parameter is connected to the ultimate prediction error by repeatedly using the chain rule. Deep learning is now feasible even for very large models because of this sophisticated mathematical process that significantly lowers computer complexity. All contemporary neural networks rely on backpropagation, which is backed by multivariable calculus and partial derivatives.

Because complicated functions sometimes consist of numerous simpler functions chained together, the chain rule itself becomes particularly potent in multivariable calculus. Artificial intelligence models generate intricately nested mathematical relationships by continually transforming data through successive computing processes. Derivatives can be calculated systematically throughout these interconnected systems using the multivariable chain rule. The chain rule enables optimization algorithms to evaluate complex models with exceptional efficiency by decomposing complex computations into digestible parts.

Second-order partial derivatives offer further insight into the behavior of functions. Second-order derivatives explain how those rates themselves vary, whereas first-order partial derivatives quantify rates of change. These higher-order derivatives reveal important properties including curvature, acceleration, and stability. Second-order information aids in distinguishing saddle points, local maxima, and local minima in optimization. Second-order notions are still useful for theoretical understanding and specialized optimization techniques, even though many real-world machine learning algorithms primarily rely on first-order derivatives for their computational efficiency.

Mixed partial derivatives look at circumstances in which differentiation happens successively about various variables. Rather than working independently, these derivatives shed light on how variables interact. Such interactions are common in real-world systems because altering one variable may affect another. Mixed partial derivatives help understand complex dependencies in mathematical representations of data, since artificial intelligence models also capture complex interactions among features.

Optimization landscapes provide another significant viewpoint on multivariable calculus. A point in a high-dimensional mathematical space corresponds to each feasible combination of model parameters. In this space, an optimization surface is defined by the loss function, with lower portions denoting more accurate models. Gradients show the sharpest ascent, whereas partial derivatives show local slopes along each coordinate direction. To navigate these landscapes, optimization algorithms follow mathematically derived paths that lead to regions with lower prediction error. This geometric perspective explains the necessity of multivariable calculus for machine learning.

Partial derivatives have several uses outside of artificial intelligence. By examining the relationships among material properties, loads, and environmental conditions, engineers optimize structural designs. Economists research the effects of investment, labor, and output on economic performance. Systems involving position, velocity, temperature, and pressure are modeled simultaneously by physicists. Medical researchers examine intricate biological systems using a variety of physiological data, while environmental scientists study the relationships between climate variables. Multivariable calculus offers consistent mathematical techniques for comprehending related phenomena across several fields.

Another real-world example is computer vision. Image recognition systems process photographs represented by matrices with thousands or millions of pixel values. While learning to recognize faces, objects, and medical anomalies, neural networks repeatedly alter these representations. Partial derivatives enable optimization algorithms to systematically improve performance by quantifying the contribution of each parameter to recognition accuracy. Similar concepts underpin autonomous driving, robotics, and voice recognition, all of which require the simultaneous analysis of multiple data sources to make trustworthy decisions.

Multivariable calculus is also crucial to natural language processing. High-dimensional mathematical vectors processed by deep neural networks are used in modern language models to represent words, phrases, and situations. Each of these networks' parameters affects language creation and comprehension. Models can enhance their grammatical recognition, contextual reasoning, translation, summarization, and conversational skills by using partial derivatives to drive optimization during training. Efficient computation of partial derivatives across large parameter fields is ultimately responsible for the extraordinary capabilities of modern language models.

Additionally, learning multivariable calculus improves general mathematical reasoning. As they realize that many real-world scenarios involve multiple interacting variables rather than isolated interactions, they develop greater respect for abstraction, logical reasoning, and systematic problem-solving. Gaining an understanding of partial derivatives allows students to thoroughly examine complex systems by considering individual influences before incorporating them into comprehensive mathematical models. Science, engineering, technology, and economics all benefit from these analytical abilities.

Even though multivariable calculus is more complicated than elementary calculus, its fundamental concepts are still based on well-known concepts of relationships and change. Gradients expand the idea of slope into higher-dimensional spaces, whereas ordinary derivatives automatically transform into partial derivatives when several variables are involved. Learners progressively gain confidence in their ability to analyze increasingly complex mathematical systems by building on previously acquired knowledge. Regular practice with computational examples, applied problems, and graphical interpretations strengthens comprehension and highlights the usefulness of these ideas.

In the end, multivariable calculus and partial derivatives provide the mathematical framework for examining and improving systems affected by numerous interacting factors. They enable researchers to train neural networks, estimate rates of change, assess parameter sensitivity, compute gradient vectors, and resolve challenging optimization problems that underpin contemporary artificial intelligence. These ideas underpin innumerable technical advancements that continue to change civilization, ranging from computer vision and natural language processing to robots, healthcare, engineering, and scientific research. Learners acquire the mathematical understanding needed to understand how intelligent systems learn from experience, improve through optimization, and make precise predictions from enormous volumes of interconnected data by mastering partial derivatives and multivariable calculus. As artificial intelligence continues to develop into more complex applications in every field of science, technology, and human activity, these potent mathematical tools will continue to be essential.

Mathematical Foundations of Neural Network Training

One of the most important cornerstones of contemporary artificial intelligence is the mathematical underpinnings of neural network training. Neural networks' real strength lies in mathematics, even though they are frequently associated with sophisticated computer science and powerful computing hardware. Every phase of neural network training relies on mathematical ideas from linear algebra, calculus, probability, optimization, and statistics, from analyzing input data and making predictions to correcting errors and improving performance. Together, these fields produce systems that can identify patterns, draw lessons from past experiences, and resolve progressively challenging issues. By understanding the mathematical underpinnings of neural network training, students can recognize that artificial intelligence is grounded in well-crafted mathematical concepts that guide learning methodically and dependably rather than on enigmatic processes.

Inspired by the structure of the human brain, a neural network is a computational model that uses mathematical formulas instead of organic neurons. Artificial neurons, the network's interconnected processing units, take numerical data, carry out computations, and generate outputs that are then transmitted to other neurons. Information can move through several levels thanks to these linkages before a final forecast is produced. Every calculation performed within a neural network adheres to exact mathematical rules that govern how information is transformed and interpreted, despite the architecture's apparent complexity.

A neural network learns from data during the training phase. At first, the network has no significant understanding of the issue it is meant to resolve. Weights and biases, two of its modifiable parameters, are given arbitrary integer values. The network's initial predictions are typically wrong because these values are random. These parameters are gradually altered throughout training, making predictions increasingly consistent with the correct responses in the training data. Repeated mathematical computations that quantify errors, identify suitable modifications, and systematically adjust parameters lead to this improvement.

Neural network calculations are structurally based on linear algebra. Vectors and matrices are used to represent each input, output, weight, and intermediary computation. A matrix arranges several vectors into rows and columns, whereas a vector is an ordered collection of numerical values that represent features. For instance, a sentence can be transformed into vectors that represent the meanings of individual words, but an image can be represented by thousands of pixel values stored within matrices. Neural networks can effectively process massive volumes of data using standardized computational techniques enabled by these mathematical frameworks.

During neural network training, one of the most common processes is matrix multiplication. After receiving input values arranged into vectors, each neuron multiplies them by the appropriate weight matrices. The final values are merged to create outputs, which are then used as inputs in other levels. Effective linear algebra is crucial for real-world artificial intelligence, as modern neural networks can perform billions of matrix multiplications during training. Because these mathematical operations are essential to machine learning, specialized computer hardware, such as graphics processing units, is made expressly to speed them up.

Weights are the numerical parameters that can be changed to control the degree to which each input affects a neuron's output. Each neuronal connection has a corresponding weight that establishes how much incoming information contributes. Certain messages are strengthened by positive weights and lessened by negative weights. To improve prediction accuracy, optimization algorithms continually adjust these weights during training. Even though individual weight variations might not seem like much, when combined, they allow neural networks to extract extremely complex patterns from massive datasets.

By enabling neurons to change their activity regardless of input values, biases offer further flexibility. Neural networks would have limited expressive power in the absence of biases, because each computation would be determined solely by the input values. By adding biases, the network's capacity to represent intricate relationships is enhanced, and neurons are better able to respond to diverse patterns. Biases are modifiable parameters that are tuned using mathematical methods throughout the training process, much like weights.

Neural networks can capture interactions that cannot be expressed by straightforward linear equations alone, thanks to activation functions, which introduce nonlinearity. Each neuron uses an activation function before generating its output after computing weighted sums of inputs. The rectified linear unit, hyperbolic tangent, and sigmoid functions are common activation functions. These mathematical functions enable networks to identify highly complex patterns by quantifying how strongly neurons respond to incoming information. No matter how many layers they had, deep neural networks would behave like straightforward linear models in the absence of nonlinear activation functions.

The way information flows through a neural network during prediction is described by forward propagation. After entering the first layer, input data goes through a series of mathematical transformations before producing outputs at the last layer. Matrix multiplication, bias addition, and activation functions collaborate methodically at each level of forward propagation. The entire procedure adheres to deterministic mathematical laws, guaranteeing consistent predictions for identical inputs even while several calculations take place concurrently.

Learning does not result from prediction alone. The neural network must assess its performance by comparing predictions with predetermined goal values after producing outputs. A loss function, which offers a numerical representation of prediction error, is used for this comparison. While a large loss shows significant discrepancies between expected and actual results, a minor loss indicates correct forecasts. Neural network training aims to reduce this loss by repeatedly adjusting weights and biases. Every training process uses this mathematical metric to guide improvement; however, the choice of suitable loss functions varies with the type of learning task.

The mathematical tools required to understand how changes in parameters affect the loss function are provided by calculus. Derivatives quantify rates of change, showing how quickly the loss rises or falls in response to changes in individual weights or biases. Partial derivatives are used to analyze the impact of each parameter independently while holding others constant because neural networks include a huge number of parameters. These derivatives provide crucial information that helps optimization algorithms identify the modifications most likely to reduce prediction errors.

Gradients are mathematical vectors that describe the direction of the loss function's greatest rise by combining partial derivatives. Optimization techniques move in the opposite direction of the gradient, since training aims to minimize prediction error rather than maximize it. Gradient descent, one of the most popular optimization methods in machine learning, is based on this procedure. Gradient descent steadily lowers the loss until the model performs satisfactorily by continually updating each configurable parameter by taking small steps in the direction opposite the gradient.

Because it dictates the magnitude of each parameter update, the learning rate is essential to gradient descent. Because updates exceed ideal solutions, optimization may become unstable if the learning rate is too high. Training progresses slowly and may require a lot of computation time if the learning rate is too low. Therefore, choosing a suitable learning rate necessitates striking a balance between stability and efficiency. To enhance convergence and overall performance, several contemporary optimization algorithms automatically adjust learning rates during training.

The mathematical process that effectively calculates gradients across neural networks is called backpropagation. Backpropagation uses the chain rule to propagate error information backward through successive layers rather than computing derivatives separately for each parameter. Derivatives are calculated layer by layer, starting with the final prediction error, until each weight and bias has a suitable gradient. Training deep neural networks with millions or billions of parameters is now feasible thanks to this effective computation, which significantly lowers computational complexity.

One of the key mathematical ideas that underpins backpropagation is the chain rule. Nested mathematical functions make up neural networks, with each layer depending on the results of the layers before it. By mixing derivatives from different stages, the chain rule provides a systematic way to compute derivatives of composite functions. Optimization methods ascertain how each parameter affects the final prediction error by repeatedly using the chain rule. It would be computationally impossible to train contemporary deep learning models without this sophisticated mathematical process.

Because neural network training frequently involves highly complex mathematical landscapes with many local minima, saddle points, and flat regions, optimization requires more than simple gradient descent. By resolving these issues, a variety of optimization strategies increase learning efficiency. Momentum reduces oscillations and accelerates convergence by incorporating prior parameter estimates. Adaptive techniques that automatically modify learning rates based on gradient behavior include AdaGrad, RMSProp, and Adam. These cutting-edge optimization methods improve training stability while reducing computational demands, enabling increasingly complex neural networks to learn efficiently from large datasets.

Neural network training also heavily relies on probability and statistics. Deterministic mathematical models are unable to adequately account for the uncertainty, measurement mistakes, and inherent variability seen in real-world data. Statistical techniques aid in the assessment of generalization performance, uncertainty estimation, and prediction accuracy. While statistical sampling approaches arrange training and testing datasets, probability distributions characterize predicted outcomes. By comprehending these ideas, researchers may create models that can produce accurate predictions even in the face of noisy or inadequate data.

Another crucial mathematical element of neural network training is regularization. Because it has learned specific details rather than broad patterns, a model that flawlessly memorizes its training examples may perform poorly when faced with new data. Regularization imposes mathematical constraints that promote simpler models with better generalization. Techniques such as weight decay, dropout, and early stopping improve performance on previously seen samples while reducing overfitting. These methods show that model complexity and predictive reliability must be balanced for learning to be successful.

The significance of mathematics in training is further demonstrated by data normalization. The various numerical scales of input features may hamper optimization. One feature might vary between zero and one, for instance, while another might vary between thousands and millions. By converting characteristics into comparable ranges, normalization enhances numerical stability and speeds up learning. By ensuring that optimization methods handle various variables more consistently, this mathematical preprocessing speeds up convergence and improves prediction accuracy.

During training, batch processing offers further computational benefits. Many neural networks employ mini-batches of manageable observations rather than waiting until the entire dataset has been analyzed or adjusting parameters after each example. Applying matrix operations to these batches preserves consistent gradient estimates while optimizing computing efficiency. Because it successfully combines speed, memory utilization, and optimization quality, mini-batch training has emerged as the standard method for contemporary deep learning.

Neural network training applications show how useful these mathematical underpinnings are in real-world situations. By identifying patterns in millions of photos, computer vision systems can identify objects. Through repeated optimization, natural language processing models can comprehend grammar, translate between languages, and produce coherent writing. Speech recognition systems use mathematical changes of audio signals to differentiate spoken words. While autonomous cars use sensor data to navigate safely, medical diagnostic technologies use image data to identify ailments. Rather than relying solely on straightforward programming instructions, all of these accomplishments rely on the mathematical principles that control neural network training.

The mathematical understanding of neural networks continues to expand through scientific research. To increase learning effectiveness and model reliability, researchers look into novel optimization algorithms, activation functions, regularization techniques, and theoretical studies. Because improved mathematical methods enable faster training, better generalization, and more accurate predictions, advances in mathematics sometimes directly lead to advancements in artificial intelligence. This intimate connection demonstrates the ongoing significance of mathematical advancement in influencing the development of intelligent technologies.

Additionally, learning about the mathematical underpinnings of neural network training enhances more general analytical thinking. Students gain a deeper understanding of abstraction, logical thinking, problem-solving, and the interdisciplinary relationships among statistics, computer science, engineering, and mathematics. Students understand artificial intelligence as a sophisticated application of basic mathematical concepts that collaborate harmoniously to solve real-world issues rather than as a collection of software tools.

In the end, the mathematical underpinnings of neural network training demonstrate that rigorous, interrelated principles underpin artificial intelligence. Calculus offers derivatives and gradients for optimization; probability and statistics handle uncertainty; linear algebra organizes data using vectors and matrices; and optimization methods methodically enhance model performance. Forward propagation, backpropagation, activation functions, loss functions, regularization, and gradient descent are some of the ideas that combine to turn unprocessed data into intelligent forecasts. These mathematical underpinnings will remain crucial to understanding how machines learn from experience and adapt to increasingly complex problems as neural networks advance healthcare, education, finance, engineering, transportation, and scientific discovery. By grasping these concepts, students acquire the knowledge needed to investigate advanced artificial intelligence, support technological advancement, and recognize the significant influence mathematics will have on the development of intelligent systems in the future.

CHAPTER IV
Probability, Statistics, and Data-Driven Intelligence

Fundamentals of Probability Theory

One of the key areas of mathematics that underpins contemporary artificial intelligence, statistics, data science, engineering, economics, and scientific research is probability theory. When total certainty is unattainable, it offers a mathematical framework for quantifying uncertainty, forecasting results, and making defensible decisions. Whether forecasting the weather, evaluating financial risks, or selecting the quickest route to a destination, people frequently make judgments in daily life based on ambiguous information. Similar difficulties arise with artificial intelligence because real-world data is frequently erratic, loud, or incomplete. Probability theory enables intelligent systems to make judgments based on available information rather than absolute certainty, estimate the likelihood of events, and evaluate uncertainty quantitatively. Learners can better understand how intelligent systems reason under uncertainty and enhance their predictions through mathematical analysis by grasping the foundations of probability theory.

The numerical indicator of an event's likelihood of happening is called probability. Every event has a probability between zero and one, with zero denoting an impossibility and one denoting complete certainty. Different levels of likelihood are indicated by values that fall between these extremes. For instance, probabilities can be used to quantify the likelihood of drawing a specific card from a standard deck, of seeing rain on a particular day, or of forecasting consumer behavior. Uncertainty is converted into quantifiable quantities through this numerical representation, which can then be examined, compared, and incorporated into computational models. Because many prediction tasks entail assessing the likelihood of multiple possible outcomes, artificial intelligence relies heavily on these assessments.

At the core of probability theory is the idea of uncertainty. Probability recognizes that many circumstances contain randomness or imperfect information, in contrast to deterministic mathematics, where identical inputs always result in similar outcomes. Because real-world settings involve numerous unknowns, intelligent systems cannot fully predict future events, even with advanced sensors and vast datasets. Instead of eliminating uncertainty, probability theory offers mathematical techniques for characterizing and controlling it. This viewpoint makes probability essential to real-world machine learning applications, as it enables artificial intelligence to make well-informed decisions even with incomplete knowledge.

Probability analysis is based on random experimentation. Any procedure whose result cannot be fully predicted before it takes place is considered a random experiment. Random experiments include rolling a die, drawing a card, tossing a coin, monitoring network traffic, and observing consumer transactions. Even when specific results are still unknown, repeated observations often reveal consistent trends that can be quantitatively described by probability theory. Data produced by comparable random processes is often analyzed by artificial intelligence, which uses probabilistic methods to identify significant patterns concealed within apparent randomness.

Each random experiment yields one or more results, which together make up the sample space. Every potential outcome that could arise during the experiment is contained in the sample space. A six-sided die, for instance, has a sample space of six possible outcomes, whereas weather forecasting includes possibilities such as sunny, overcast, or wet conditions. Calculating probabilities consistently is made possible for mathematicians and machine learning practitioners by clearly specifying the sample space. Similar to this, artificial intelligence first determines potential prediction categories before assessing the probabilities of those categories.

A particular set of results within the sample area is called an event. While some events have only one possible outcome, others have several. An event with multiple possible outcomes, for example, is represented by rolling an even number on a die. Events are also a part of machine learning classification tasks, including identifying whether an email is spam or whether a medical imaging shows a disease. Based on observed data and mathematical reasoning, probability theory offers methodical ways to assign numerical likelihoods to these occurrences.

When all possible events are equally likely, classical probability provides one of the most straightforward methods for computing probabilities. In these circumstances, probability is calculated by dividing the number of favorable outcomes by the total number of possible outcomes. Classical probability offers useful intuition about chance and unpredictability, even if many real-world scenarios have uneven probabilities. These concepts are frequently extended by artificial intelligence to more complicated scenarios where probabilities must be calculated from seen data rather than presumed to be uniformly distributed.

By estimating probabilities through repeated observations, experimental probability takes a new approach to uncertainty. Experimental probability quantifies the frequency of events throughout repeated trials rather than depending just on theoretical computations. Experimental estimates frequently approach the underlying theoretical probability as the number of observations increases. Similar ideas apply to machine learning since models do not rely solely on presumptions, but rather learn probability distributions directly from vast datasets. Artificial intelligence can continuously improve its forecasting accuracy and adapt to new environments thanks to this data-driven methodology.

Because it explains how probabilities change when new information becomes available, conditional probability is one of the most powerful concepts in probability theory. Many decisions made in the real world are based on pertinent evidence observed in advance, as well as on rare incidents. For instance, although the likelihood of a medical problem depends on diagnostic test results, the risk of rain increases once dark clouds are observed. Conditional probability is essential to intelligent decision-making because artificial intelligence regularly modifies predictions in response to new information. AI systems provide more precise, context-sensitive predictions by mathematically incorporating evidence.

Independent events provide another key idea in probability theory. If the occurrence of one event does not affect the likelihood of the other, then the two events are said to be independent. Because past results have no bearing on subsequent flips, tossing a coin several times demonstrates independence. To simplify mathematical analysis and improve computational efficiency, many machine learning models assume that some variables are independent of one another. Even though total independence is rare in complex real-world datasets, understanding this concept can help with algorithm design and probabilistic modeling.

On the other hand, dependent events happen when one event affects the likelihood of another. Weather, financial markets, consumer purchasing patterns, and medical diagnoses all frequently entail intricate relationships between variables. Because assuming independence in situations where dependencies exist can reduce prediction accuracy, artificial intelligence models often need to account for these dependencies. By modeling these interactions mathematically, probability theory enables intelligent systems to recognize realistic patterns in observable data.

The likelihood of two or more events occurring simultaneously is examined using joint probability. Because several factors often affect predictions simultaneously, this idea is particularly crucial in artificial intelligence. When making navigation judgments, autonomous vehicles, for instance, consider the joint probability of traffic lights, pedestrian activity, and road conditions. Joint probabilities that describe the links between consumers, products, and preferences are analyzed by recommendation systems. AI systems enhance decision-making across a variety of real-world applications by mathematically modeling interdependencies among events.

Probability distributions provide comprehensive explanations of how probabilities are distributed across potential outcomes. Distributions summarize the behavior of complete random variables rather than concentrating on individual events. Continuous probability distributions apply to measurements that can take an unlimited number of values, whereas discrete probability distributions apply to scenarios with countable outcomes. Probability distributions that characterize consumer behavior, image attributes, financial hazards, and biological measures are often estimated using machine learning algorithms. By understanding these distributions, intelligent systems can forecast patterns rather than individual data points.

Uncertain quantities are represented mathematically by random variables. Random variables simplify probability analysis and statistical modeling by assigning numerical values to potential events rather than explicitly recording outcomes. Because numerical representations make mathematical computation easier, uncertain aspects are often represented by artificial intelligence as random variables. In machine learning models, weights, temperatures, incomes, sensor readings, and prediction scores all naturally behave as random variables.

By showing the long-term average result of a random variable over numerous repeated trials, expected value offers another key idea. The expected value quantifies the average outcome expected given the same conditions, despite the unpredictability of individual observations. When assessing choices, projecting future benefits, and refining forecasts, artificial intelligence heavily relies on expected values. For instance, rather than ensuring immediate success, reinforcement learning algorithms seek actions that maximize expected future rewards. This mathematical viewpoint enables intelligent systems to strike a balance between long-term performance and unpredictability.

The degree to which data deviate from their predicted values is measured by variance and standard deviation. Variance measures uncertainty by showing the range of potential outcomes, whereas anticipated value describes central tendency. Greater unpredictability is reflected in high variation, while more consistent behavior is indicated by low variance. To assess data quality, identify anomalies, and gauge prediction reliability, machine learning algorithms analyze variance. By comprehending variability, researchers can enhance model resilience and differentiate significant patterns from random fluctuations.

By focusing on learning from evidence, Bayesian probability expands on classical probability. Bayesian approaches update beliefs as new information becomes available, as opposed to regarding probability as fixed numbers. Because humans naturally adjust their expectations in response to new information, this method is quite similar to human thinking. Bayesian techniques are widely used in artificial intelligence for scientific inference, robotics, natural language processing, medical diagnosis, and recommendation systems. The way that probability theory facilitates adaptive learning in uncertain situations is illustrated by Bayesian reasoning.

Additionally, probability is essential to supervised machine learning. Classification algorithms often estimate probabilities indicating how likely data are to fall into certain categories. Probabilistic models provide confidence levels that represent forecast uncertainty rather than straightforward yes-or-no responses. An image recognition system might, for instance, assign lower probabilities to other categories while estimating a 98% probability that an object is a bicycle. Users can assess prediction reliability and make well-informed decisions based on model confidence using these probability estimates.

Probability theory also helps unsupervised learning. To find natural groupings within datasets, clustering algorithms often estimate probabilistic correlations among observations. By allowing data to belong partially to multiple groups, probabilistic clustering recognizes uncertainty rather than imposing strict boundaries. The intricacy of many real-world datasets, in which categories overlap rather than remain entirely distinct, is better captured by this adaptable mathematical method.

Another interesting use of probability theory is in natural language processing. Because words can have numerous meanings depending on context, human language contains a great deal of ambiguity. By estimating the probability of various word sequences, probabilistic language models enable systems to produce coherent sentences, translate between languages, recognize speech, and provide accurate answers to queries. Probability distributions characterizing linguistic patterns acquired from massive text collections are a key component of all contemporary conversational AI systems.

Probability is also a major component of computer vision. While accounting for uncertainty due to illumination, shifting viewpoints, and image quality, image recognition systems assess the probability that visual features belong to specific objects. Before choosing safe courses of action, autonomous cars assess the likelihood of surrounding objects, road conditions, and potential hazards. Medical imaging technologies help medical professionals diagnose and arrange treatments by estimating disease probability based on visual evidence.

Reinforcement learning, in which intelligent creatures learn by interacting with unpredictable surroundings, is further aided by probability theory. Because external variables are constantly changing, actions rarely ensure the same results. To balance the exploration of new possibilities against the exploitation of existing information, reinforcement learning algorithms assess the probability associated with future rewards. With experience, intelligent systems can steadily enhance their performance through this probabilistic decision-making process.

Additionally, learning probability theory enhances more general analytical thinking. While realizing that many real-world issues cannot be resolved by deterministic approaches alone, learners gain a deeper understanding of uncertainty, evidence-based reasoning, and quantitative decision-making. Probability promotes realistic risk assessment, rigorous analysis of forecasts, and cautious interpretation of data. These mental abilities remain useful across a wide range of fields, including public policy, research, engineering, healthcare, and finance.

In the end, probability theory's foundations offer a crucial mathematical basis for contemporary data science and artificial intelligence. Probability helps intelligent systems assess incomplete data, estimate possible outcomes, update predictions based on facts, and make well-informed judgments in uncertain situations by quantifying uncertainty. Strong mathematical frameworks supporting machine learning, computer vision, natural language processing, robotics, healthcare, finance, and scientific research are built by combining concepts such as random experiments, sample spaces, events, conditional probability, independence, probability distributions, expected value, variance, and Bayesian reasoning. Probability theory will continue to be essential for understanding uncertainty, improving prediction accuracy, and creating intelligent systems that reason effectively in an unpredictable world as artificial intelligence advances into more complex applications.

Statistical Measures and Data Interpretation

The key elements of mathematics that allow individuals to convert unprocessed data into useful knowledge are statistical measurements and data interpretation. Business transactions, scientific research, healthcare systems, social media platforms, financial markets, educational institutions, and artificial intelligence applications all produce massive volumes of information every second in today's data-driven world. However, without careful organization, analysis, and interpretation, raw data is not very valuable on its own. The mathematical techniques required to assess variance, identify trends, summarize complex datasets, and support evidence-based decision-making are provided by statistics. Because machine learning models must analyze vast amounts of data, identify significant associations, assess prediction accuracy, and continuously adjust based on observed information, artificial intelligence relies heavily on statistical principles. Gaining an understanding of statistical measurements and data interpretation provides students with the mathematical foundation they need to create dependable, effective, and intelligent computing systems.

The area of mathematics known as statistics deals with gathering, organizing, analyzing, interpreting, and presenting data. In contrast to basic arithmetic, which concentrates on single numerical computations, statistics looks at collections of observations to find patterns and connections that might not be immediately apparent. Statistical techniques uncover more comprehensive patterns that bolster well-informed judgments by examining data sets rather than individual values. Because machine learning algorithms enhance their effectiveness by finding statistical regularities within vast datasets rather than memorizing specific examples, artificial intelligence heavily relies on these techniques.

Gathering trustworthy data is the initial stage in statistical analysis. Accurate data gathering is crucial because high-quality conclusions rely on high-quality information. Surveys, experiments, sensors, financial records, medical observations, consumer contacts, and digital systems are some of the sources of data. Data collected from cameras, microphones, wearables, internet transactions, and scientific instruments is often processed by artificial intelligence. Subsequent statistical analysis and machine learning predictions may be incorrect if the acquired data contains substantial errors, missing values, or biases. Consequently, the basis of any effective statistical study is meticulous data gathering.

Before effective analysis can start, data must be arranged after collection. Researchers and intelligent systems can analyze observations more effectively by organizing data into tables, categories, databases, or structured datasets. Typically, machine learning models use matrices to represent datasets, with rows representing observations and columns representing features or variables. This structured framework simplifies statistical computations and enables algorithms to compare observations systematically. An effective organization also makes it easier to spot anomalies, outliers, and missing data that may require further research before the model is developed.

The measure of central tendency is among the most basic ideas in statistics. Central tendency offers a succinct overview of several observations by describing the typical or representative value within a sample. Analysts frequently look for a single value that reflects the overall behavior of the entire collection rather than looking at each piece of data individually. The mean, median, and mode are the three main measures of central tendency frequently used. Depending on the data's features, each serves distinct analytical functions and offers insightful information.

By adding all the observations and dividing by the number of values, one can determine the arithmetic mean, often known as the average. Because it condenses all observations into a single numerical measure, the mean offers a helpful summary when the data is reasonably balanced. When preprocessing data, artificial intelligence often employs mean values to replace missing observations, standardize characteristics, and summarize big datasets. Even though the mean is important, unusually large or small values can substantially affect it, necessitating additional statistical measures for a more thorough interpretation.

When observations are ordered numerically, the median is the midway value. The median is especially helpful for datasets with abnormally high or low observations since, in contrast to the mean, it is largely unaffected by extreme values. Medical costs, housing costs, and income distributions frequently exhibit skewed distributions, with median values providing more accurate representations than averages. To identify asymmetry in datasets and select appropriate analytical methods, machine learning practitioners often compare means and medians.

The mode identifies the value that appears most frequently in a dataset. The mode, which is often overlooked in favor of the mean and median, offers important insights into typical values, especially when examining categorical data. Because determining the most prevalent category aids corporate decision-making and recommendation systems, modal analysis frequently informs customer purchasing preferences, product selections, and survey responses. Similar to this, artificial intelligence recognizes recurrent patterns in seen data by utilizing modal information.

A dataset cannot be well described by measures of central tendency alone since observations can differ significantly even when averages are identical. Therefore, measures of dispersion offer more details about the spread or variability. These statistics assist analysts in evaluating consistency, predictability, and uncertainty by quantifying the degree to which observations deviate from one another. Because excessive variation may indicate noisy data, anomalous observations, or complex underlying relationships that require specialist analysis, machine learning models rely heavily on an understanding of variability.

One of the most basic ways to quantify dispersion is the range. It provides a basic indicator of overall dispersion and is computed by deducting the smallest observation from the greatest. Although simple to calculate, the range may not adequately capture the variability of the remaining observations because it depends only on two extreme values. However, exposing major disparities between datasets, providing helpful initial insight during exploratory data analysis.

By computing the average squared departure of observations from the mean, variance offers a more thorough measure of dispersion. While highlighting greater disparities, squaring deviations guarantees that positive and negative differences contribute equally. Because many optimization methods and statistical models directly rely on variance calculations, variance is particularly significant in machine learning. Greater variability across observations is indicated by high variance, whereas more consistent data patterns are shown by low variance.

By expressing variability in the same units as the original data, standard deviation—which is derived from variance—makes interpretation easier to understand. While a big standard deviation indicates significant dispersion, a small standard deviation shows that observations are closely clustered around the mean. Artificial intelligence systems often use standard deviation analysis to assess feature significance, detect anomalies, and gauge prediction uncertainty. Researchers can differentiate between random fluctuations and steady patterns in observed data by comprehending standard deviation.

Additional techniques for describing data distributions include percentiles and quartiles. These measurements show how data is distributed across different ranges by dividing observations into meaningful intervals rather than focusing solely on core values. Whereas percentiles split datasets into 100 equal parts, quartiles split them into 4 equal parts. To compare individual observations with larger populations, percentile-based interpretations are frequently used in educational testing, healthcare evaluations, financial analysis, and machine learning assessments.

Data distributions offer a crucial background for statistical interpretation and characterize the general form of observed data. While some datasets show skewed distributions with lengthy tails extending toward abnormally large or tiny values, others follow roughly symmetrical patterns where observations cluster equally around the mean. Analysts can choose the best statistical methods and identify significant associations by having a solid understanding of the data distribution. Accurate distributional analysis is crucial for trustworthy predictions, as artificial intelligence algorithms often assume specific probability distributions during model construction.

Because graphical representations frequently highlight trends that numerical summaries alone could miss, visualization is crucial to the interpretation of data. Analysts can identify trends, clusters, outliers, and correlations between variables with the aid of histograms, scatter plots, box plots, line graphs, and other visualizations. Before building machine learning models, artificial intelligence practitioners frequently conduct exploratory data analysis using visual techniques. While enhancing the overall quality of the model, these visual insights often direct feature selection, preprocessing choices, and algorithm selection.

The degree and direction of links between variables are measured by correlation. While a negative correlation implies that one variable falls as the other rises, a positive correlation indicates that the variables tend to rise together. The degree of relationship is described numerically by correlation coefficients, which range from negative to positive. Strongly connected variables may provide useful predictive information or introduce redundancy that needs careful management. Machine learning algorithms often rely on correlations when selecting relevant features.

Differentiating between correlation and causality is crucial. Strong statistical correlations between two variables might exist even when one does not directly cause the other. Apparent correlations may result from indirect linkages, chance happenstance, or shared underlying factors. Careful interpretation is crucial, as artificial intelligence models primarily detect statistical patterns rather than causal mechanisms. Before making conclusions about cause-and-effect correlations, researchers must integrate statistical evidence with domain expertise.

Observations that significantly deviate from the bulk of the data are known as outliers. Measurement errors, uncommon occurrences, or truly significant phenomena could be the cause of these strange results. Because extreme observations can skew averages, variances, and correlations, and degrade machine learning performance, identifying outliers is an essential part of statistical analysis. Specialized algorithms for spotting irregularities in financial transactions, medical diagnosis, cybersecurity monitoring, and industrial quality control are frequently found in artificial intelligence systems. Whether outliers should be investigated, corrected, or retained for further study depends on how they are interpreted.

Before machine learning models begin training, data preprocessing relies heavily on statistical measures. Means, medians, or more complex statistical estimations can be used to replace missing values. To guarantee consistent numerical scales, features are often standardized or normalized using statistical summaries. Statistical filtering is used in noise-reduction techniques to enhance data quality. By supplying cleaner, more consistent input data, these preprocessing steps increase model stability, accelerate optimization, and improve forecast accuracy.

Evaluation of machine learning models also heavily relies on statistical interpretation. Prediction quality across testing datasets is summarized using performance metrics such as accuracy, precision, recall, and error rates. While cross-validation evaluates model generalization across several data partitions, confidence intervals estimate the uncertainty surrounding evaluation outcomes. Statistical evaluation uses systematic mathematical techniques to analyze overall performance instead of depending on individual predictions. This thorough evaluation ensures that intelligent systems operate consistently when presented with previously unseen data.

Numerous instances of statistical interpretation supporting AI applications may be found in the healthcare industry. To identify disease trends, assess treatment efficacy, and forecast health outcomes, medical researchers analyze patient data. Laboratory data are summarized, disease development is tracked, and diagnostic accuracy is estimated using statistical methods. While acknowledging the ambiguity inherent in medical decision-making, machine learning models trained on statistically evaluated datasets help doctors by providing evidence-based recommendations.

Statistical metrics are also essential to business analytics. Businesses use descriptive statistics and prediction models to analyze consumer purchase patterns, product demand, marketing effectiveness, and financial trends. Artificial intelligence systems analyze these datasets to estimate sales, optimize inventories, tailor recommendations, and boost operational effectiveness. Large datasets of company data are transformed into useful insights that drive competitive advantage and strategic planning through statistical analysis.

Statistical analysis is also used in scientific studies in many different fields. Environmental scientists track climate trends, economists' study financial indicators, engineers assess system reliability, and social scientists use statistical techniques to examine human behavior. These domains are increasingly enhanced by artificial intelligence, which identifies minute patterns in complex information that conventional analysis might miss. This collaboration between machine learning and statistics improves the validity of scientific findings while accelerating discovery.

Gaining statistical literacy enhances critical thinking in areas other than mathematics. Students improve their ability to evaluate numerical assertions, spot deceptive interpretations, evaluate the facts objectively, and make well-informed decisions in the face of uncertainty. These analytical abilities are still useful in education, the workplace, public policy, healthcare, finance, engineering, and daily life. Rather than accepting numerical data without examination, an understanding of statistical reasoning promotes careful interpretation.

Statistical measurements and data interpretation ultimately provide the mathematical basis for transforming raw data into meaningful knowledge. Measures of central tendency summarize typical values; measures of dispersion quantify variability; linkages are identified by correlation; probability distributions describe patterns; and hidden structures within complex datasets are revealed through visualization. When combined, these ideas allow artificial intelligence systems to methodically examine data, identify significant patterns, assess the accuracy of predictions, and make trustworthy decisions even in the face of uncertainty. Statistical reasoning will continue to be essential for scientific research, technological innovation, corporate intelligence, and artificial intelligence as data continues to rise in volume and significance across all facets of contemporary society. By grasping these fundamental ideas, students gain the mathematical knowledge required to analyze data accurately, critically assess evidence, and support the ongoing development of intelligent systems that can solve increasingly challenging real-world problems.

Probability Distributions and Statistical Inference

Two of the most crucial mathematical ideas that underpin contemporary artificial intelligence, machine learning, data science, and scientific inquiry are probability distributions and statistical inference. Information from the real world is rarely flawless or entirely predictable. Unexpected changes in the weather, volatile financial markets, unclear medical diagnoses, and situational variations in human behavior are all common. Probability and statistics are crucial mathematical techniques because artificial intelligence systems must function well despite these uncertainties. While statistical inference enables inferences about bigger populations from limited observations, probability distributions reflect the likelihood of various occurrences. When combined, these ideas offer a mathematical framework that helps intelligent systems examine data, calculate uncertainty, forecast outcomes, and make better decisions based on facts rather than conjecture.

The assignment of probabilities to the potential values of a random variable is described mathematically by a probability distribution. A probability distribution accounts for all conceivable outcomes and their probabilities, rather than just one. This all-encompassing perspective enables researchers and intelligent systems to comprehend not only potential outcomes but also the likelihood of each alternative. Because probability distributions provide a structured way to represent imperfect knowledge and facilitate well-informed decision-making, they are frequently used in artificial intelligence to model uncertainty.

The result of a random operation is represented numerically by a random variable. Temperatures, test results, customer sales, medical test results, and sensor readings are just a few examples of the kinds of information that can be modeled as random variables. Many input features and prediction outputs are regarded as random variables in machine learning because their values vary between observations. Instead of relying on predetermined assumptions, algorithms can use statistical techniques and probability theory to analyze patterns when unknown values are modeled mathematically.

Discrete distributions and continuous distributions are the two primary categories into which probability distributions are typically divided. The number of damaged products in a shipment or the number of customers entering a business during a particular hour are examples of scenarios where probable outcomes may be enumerated individually and are described by discrete probability distributions. Continuous probability distributions apply to measurements such as height, weight, temperature, and time that can take any value within a range. Depending on the features of the data being examined, artificial intelligence systems can operate with both kinds of distributions. The accuracy and dependability of mathematical models are enhanced by choosing the right distribution.

The normal distribution is one of the most popular probability distributions. The symmetrical bell-shaped curve that characterizes the normal distribution shows that fewer observations appear farther from the center and that the majority of observations cluster around the average value. Measurement mistakes, test scores, biological traits, and some financial variables are only a few examples of the many natural and artificial occurrences that roughly follow this distribution. The normal distribution is crucial in statistics and machine learning because of its mathematical properties and its prevalence in real-world data. When developing models and preparing data, many methods assume that the data is roughly normal.

Expected value is another key concept in probability distributions. If an experiment is repeated numerous times under the same circumstances, the expected value is the long-term average result of a random variable. Even if randomness causes individual observations to differ, the expected value provides a reliable summary of overall behavior. Expected values are used by artificial intelligence in decision-making, prediction, and optimization. For instance, rather than concentrating only on current results, reinforcement learning chooses actions that maximize anticipated future benefits.

The degree of variability within a probability distribution is measured by variance and standard deviation. Variance shows how broadly observations are distributed about a distribution's center, whereas the expected value describes the distribution's core. The standard deviation makes understanding easier by expressing this spread in the same units as the original data. Low variance denotes more consistent observations, whereas high variance implies more uncertainty. When assessing features, identifying anomalous observations, and calculating prediction confidence, machine learning algorithms examine variance.

Theoretical probability and real-world statistical analysis are connected through sampling. Studying the entire population is often not feasible due to the high time, expense, or resource requirements. Rather, to evaluate the characteristics of the larger population, researchers gather representative samples. Similar methods are used by artificial intelligence, which learns from available training data rather than seeing every possible example. Good sampling techniques help machine learning models generalize to new data and increase the validity of statistical conclusions.

Making inferences about a population using data gathered from a sample is known as statistical inference. Inference goes beyond observed values to estimate unknown features and make predictions rather than only characterizing acquired facts. Similar logic is used by artificial intelligence to identify patterns in past data and apply those patterns to new circumstances. The mathematical concepts that enable intelligent systems to make meaningful predictions even when little information is available are provided by statistical inference.

One of the main objectives of statistical inference is parameter estimation. Averages, probabilities, and measures of variability are population characteristics that must be estimated from sample data because they are often unknown. Whereas interval estimates give ranges that are likely to contain the actual population parameters, point estimates give single numerical values. Confidence intervals are particularly useful since they show how accurate an estimate is while acknowledging uncertainty. Confidence estimates are increasingly incorporated into forecasts by artificial intelligence, enabling consumers to assess the reliability of model outputs.

Another significant use of statistical inference is hypothesis testing. To ascertain whether the observed evidence supports a hypothesis about a relationship or difference in the data, researchers frequently begin by formulating a hypothesis. To compare algorithms, assess novel approaches, and determine whether reported advances are statistically significant rather than due to chance, machine learning researchers employ hypothesis testing. This procedure helps ensure that conclusions are supported by data rather than by chance.

By fusing previously known information with recently discovered data, Bayesian inference provides an alternate method to statistical reasoning. Bayesian approaches use probability distributions that vary as new information becomes available to represent uncertain quantities rather than treating them as fixed values. Because people naturally modify their views in response to new information, this method is similar to human learning. Bayesian inference is used by artificial intelligence in a variety of applications where ongoing learning and adaptation are necessary, such as robots, medical diagnosis, recommendation systems, and natural language processing.

Additionally, probability distributions are essential for machine learning classification. Many algorithms assess the likelihood that an observation belongs to each potential class rather than simply classifying observations. An image recognition system might determine, for instance, that a photograph has a 98% chance of including a bicycle and a substantially lower chance of containing other things. These probability estimates enable users to assess the certainty of model judgments and offer useful information on prediction confidence.

Another application of probability distributions is found in natural language processing. Because words and sentences can have multiple meanings depending on the context, human language is ambiguous. Language models use patterns discovered in vast text collections to calculate the likelihood of certain word sequences. Artificial intelligence systems can produce coherent answers, translate languages, summarize materials, and provide remarkably accurate answers by choosing the most likely sentence continuation.

Probabilistic reasoning is also a major component of computer vision. Perfect recognition is challenging because images sometimes contain shadows, noise, dim lighting, or partially obscured objects. Instead of assuming total certainty, artificial intelligence systems estimate probability distributions characterizing potential object identities. Before making navigation decisions, autonomous vehicles assess the likelihood of pedestrians, traffic signs, road conditions, and nearby vehicles. In unpredictable situations, this probabilistic method increases dependability and safety.

Additionally, scientific research, healthcare, finance, engineering, and environmental studies all benefit from probability distributions and statistical inference. Environmental scientists use statistical models to forecast climate trends, engineers assess system reliability, economists use probability distributions to examine financial risks, and medical researchers use statistical inference to determine treatment effectiveness. By evaluating large amounts of information, identifying trends, and generating predictions using probabilistic reasoning, artificial intelligence enhances performance across various domains.

To sum up, statistical inference and probability distributions provide the mathematical underpinnings for understanding uncertainty and drawing well-informed conclusions from data. While statistical inference enables drawing meaningful conclusions from representative samples, probability distributions characterize the likelihood of certain events. Artificial intelligence systems may learn from experience, assess uncertainty, and improve prediction accuracy through concepts such as random variables, expected value, variance, sampling, confidence intervals, hypothesis testing, and Bayesian inference. These mathematical concepts will remain essential for creating intelligent systems that reason well, adapt to changing circumstances, and make trustworthy decisions based on evidence rather than certainty as artificial intelligence continues to spread across healthcare, finance, education, transportation, scientific research, and countless other domains.

Managing Uncertainty in Artificial Intelligence Systems

One of the most significant issues in the development and functioning of artificial intelligence systems is managing uncertainty. Artificial intelligence frequently operates in contexts where information is fragmentary, noisy, constantly changing, or intrinsically ambiguous, in contrast to traditional computer programs that adhere to set instructions and generate predictable outputs for identical inputs. Without a perfect understanding of every scenario they encounter, intelligent systems must make decisions. Artificial intelligence must assess ambiguous information and choose the best course of action, whether it is used for image recognition, spoken language comprehension, product recommendations, illness diagnosis, or autonomous vehicle guidance. Effective uncertainty management is grounded in mathematics, particularly probability theory, statistics, optimization, and decision theory. Knowing these mathematical concepts makes it easier to understand how artificial intelligence systems can draw trustworthy conclusions even in situations where certainty is difficult to achieve.

When full information is not known or future events cannot be accurately foreseen, uncertainty is present. When making financial decisions, selecting medical treatments, or checking weather forecasts, people deal with uncertainty daily. Because real-world data rarely offers total assurance, artificial intelligence encounters comparable challenges. Shadows may be present in images, sensors may yield erroneous measurements, customer preferences may evolve, and human language frequently contains ambiguity. Artificial intelligence uses mathematical techniques to estimate probabilities and assess confidence before making decisions, rather than ignoring these uncertainties.

Incomplete data is one of the main reasons artificial intelligences is unsure. Examples gathered from user interactions, experiments, observations, and sensor readings are used to train machine learning models. Nevertheless, no dataset can cover every scenario a system may encounter. Due to insufficient observations, unavailable measurements, or shifting surroundings, some information can be absent. A recommendation system might be aware of only a subset of a customer's interests, whereas a medical diagnosis system might examine patient records that do not include every laboratory result. Therefore, even with incomplete information, artificial intelligence must produce meaningful predictions.

Another significant source of uncertainty is measurement inaccuracy. Environmental sensors, medical equipment, cameras, microphones, and satellites are not entirely accurate. Temperature sensors may produce small errors, microphones may record undesired background sounds, and images may contain visual disturbances. These flaws impact the quality of the data that artificial intelligence systems can access. Despite faulty observations, intelligent systems can generate more accurate predictions thanks to statistical techniques that help separate relevant patterns from measurement errors.

One of the best mathematical tools for handling uncertainty is probability theory. Probability provides numerical values that indicate the likelihood of various outcomes rather than assuming that forecasts are always accurate. These probabilities range from 1, which denotes total confidence, to 0, which represents impossible outcomes. These probability values are used by artificial intelligence to compare potential outcomes and calculate prediction confidence. An image recognition model might, for instance, assign substantially lower probabilities to other objects while estimating a 97% probability that an image contains a bicycle. Users can better understand the degree of confidence associated with each forecast thanks to these probability estimates.

By representing the likelihood of each possible outcome rather than focusing on a single prediction, probability distributions build on this concept. Probability distributions offer a comprehensive mathematical representation of uncertainty as opposed to making a single judgment without justification. These distributions are used in a variety of artificial intelligence applications, including recommendation systems, computer vision, speech recognition, and financial forecasting. Intelligent systems become more adaptable and better equipped to respond as new information becomes available by considering multiple options simultaneously.

Another useful method for handling uncertainty is Bayesian reasoning. Every time new information is discovered, Bayesian techniques update probability estimates. Bayesian inference enables intelligent systems to update their findings as new information becomes available, rather than accepting predictions as final. Because humans naturally modify their ideas after absorbing new information, this method resembles human reasoning. For instance, laboratory test findings bolster the confidence of medical diagnostic systems, and as sensors continuously gather new data, autonomous cars improve their understanding of road conditions.

By itself, machine learning is a useful technique for lowering uncertainty through experience. Algorithms examine large datasets during training to identify patterns and relationships that improve prediction accuracy. Models improve their ability to identify significant structures within complex information by fine-tuning their internal parameters as more data becomes available. Artificial intelligence may learn from experience and make more dependable decisions over time while adapting to changing environments, even when uncertainty cannot be eliminated.

Uncertainty management also heavily relies on statistical inference. Artificial intelligence learns from representative samples since whole populations are rarely accessible for analysis. Mathematical methods for estimating population characteristics and assessing the validity of conclusions are provided by statistical inference. Instead of disregarding uncertainty, parameter estimation, hypothesis testing, and confidence intervals help quantify it. By using these techniques, intelligent systems can convey not only their predictions but also the degree of confidence that accompanies them.

In contemporary artificial intelligence, confidence estimation has become increasingly significant. Alongside their predictions, many sophisticated systems generate confidence scores that let users assess how certain the model is about its findings. For example, in the medical field, an AI system may diagnose a medical issue with a high degree of confidence or suggest further testing if the confidence level is low. By assisting users in identifying circumstances that require additional research or human monitoring, similar confidence estimates enhance decision-making in cybersecurity, finance, manufacturing, and transportation.

By enhancing the learning process, optimization strategies provide further support for uncertainty management. To minimize prediction errors while retaining the ability to perform effectively on new data, machine learning algorithms adjust their parameters during training. Because it has learned random details rather than significant patterns, a model that memorizes training examples may perform badly in novel scenarios. By pushing models to learn general relationships rather than memorize particular examples, regularization techniques help avoid this issue. When there is ambiguity, this balance increases reliability.

Applications of artificial intelligence highlight the significance of uncertainty management in a variety of industries. Before determining how to brake, accelerate, or steer safely, autonomous cars must assess ambiguous data from cameras, radar, and lidar sensors. Rather than making firm judgments, diagnostic methods use laboratory tests, medical imaging, and clinical symptoms to assess the likelihood of a condition. Financial institutions use probabilistic models to assess investment risks and identify fraudulent transactions. Given insufficient preference data, recommendation systems estimate the probability that consumers will like specific goods or services. In all situations, artificial intelligence can function more successfully in challenging real-world settings thanks to uncertainty management.

The importance of uncertainty is further illustrated by natural language processing. Sentence interpretation frequently depends on context, and many words in human language have numerous meanings. Before choosing the best interpretation, artificial intelligence models calculate the probability for various word sequences and meanings. Despite the ambiguity of human language, this probabilistic reasoning enables conversational systems, translation software, and text-generation models to produce coherent, contextually accurate responses.

Uncertainty management and ethical issues are closely related. Instead of portraying uncertain predictions as solid facts, artificial intelligence systems should be honest in their communication of ambiguity. Particularly in applications related to public safety, criminal justice, healthcare, or education, users must be aware of the limitations and confidence of automated decisions. When necessary, adequate human oversight is encouraged, and responsible decision-making is supported by transparent disclosure of uncertainty. To reduce prejudice, promote justice, and ensure that intelligent systems remain reliable, developers must also carefully assess uncertainty.

To manage uncertainty, human skill remains crucial. Even if artificial intelligence is capable of rapidly analyzing enormous volumes of data, human judgment is still useful for deciphering peculiar circumstances, taking ethical considerations into account, and reaching conclusions in difficult scenarios. The most successful systems combine human oversight with mathematical reasoning, enabling artificial intelligence to provide evidence-based recommendations while, when necessary, delegating crucial choices to qualified experts.

In conclusion, as real-world settings are rarely comprehensive or predictable, handling uncertainty is an essential component of artificial intelligence. Intelligent systems learn to assess uncertainty and make well-informed judgments based on available data through probability theory, statistical inference, Bayesian reasoning, optimization, confidence estimation, and machine learning. While acknowledging the constraints of the knowledge at hand, these mathematical strategies enable artificial intelligence to communicate confidence, enhance forecast accuracy, and adapt to changing conditions. Effective uncertainty management will remain crucial for developing dependable, transparent, and trustworthy intelligent systems capable of addressing increasingly complex real-world challenges as artificial intelligence spreads across healthcare, transportation, finance, education, manufacturing, and scientific research.

CHAPTER V
Advanced Mathematical Frameworks for Modern Artificial Intelligence

Discrete Mathematics and Graph Theory

Computer science, artificial intelligence, data science, cybersecurity, software engineering, and many other technology-driven professions rely heavily on discrete mathematics and graph theory as their mathematical underpinning. Discrete mathematics is concerned with discrete, distinct, and countable objects, in contrast to continuous mathematics, which examines values that can fluctuate smoothly across an infinite range. Integers, logical assertions, sets, sequences, trees, graphs, and finite structures that are amenable to exact mathematical analysis are among them. Discrete mathematics naturally provides the language and structure for understanding computational systems, since computers handle digital information in discrete units such as bits and bytes rather than continuous values. One of the most effective tools for creating intelligent systems is graph theory, a significant area of discrete mathematics that provides techniques for representing relationships among objects. When combined, these branches of mathematics enable artificial intelligence to support intelligent decision-making across a wide range of real-world applications, organize information, solve complex problems, and analyze interconnected data.

The focus on finite structures in discrete mathematics is one of its distinguishing features. Discrete mathematics examines items that may be counted separately as opposed to dealing with infinitely divisible numbers. Whole numbers, computer memory locations, network connections, logical values, and item combinations are a few examples. Because digital systems inherently use finite representations of information, discrete mathematics is especially well-suited to computing. When organizing information, creating search strategies, assessing logical conditions, and describing knowledge, artificial intelligence algorithms usually rely on discrete mathematical ideas. These mathematical ideas guarantee the accuracy, efficiency, and logical consistency of computer procedures.

One of the essential components of discrete mathematics is set theory. A well-defined collection of unique items, arranged according to particular attributes, is called a set. These items might stand in for almost any identifying entity, including numbers, persons, documents, pictures, and goods. Mathematical techniques for comparing and combining sets of data include set operations like union, intersection, difference, and complement. Database administration, feature selection, categorization, recommendation systems, and knowledge representation are just a few of the many uses of set theory in artificial intelligence. Intelligent systems can efficiently extract relevant data and organize information systematically by understanding relationships between sets.

Another crucial element of discrete mathematics is mathematical logic. Logic examines claims as either true or false and assesses how reliably conclusions can be drawn from known information. Decision-making, rule evaluation, automated reasoning, and program verification are all based on logical reasoning. Expert systems, knowledge-based systems, automated theorem proving, and reasoning engines that can derive conclusions from accessible data are all supported by logical approaches in artificial intelligence. Logical reasoning remains essential whenever systems need to justify their choices, adhere to clear guidelines, or verify accuracy, even though many contemporary AI methods place a strong emphasis on statistical learning.

Using logical operators such as conjunction, disjunction, negation, implication, and equivalence, propositional logic introduces students to the mathematical representation of statements. These operators maintain exact logical relationships while enabling the combination of simple assertions into more complicated expressions. Truth tables provide systematic methods for assessing all possible logical combinations of values, ensuring that conclusions hold across many situations. When assessing circumstances, applying decision rules, verifying software, and creating automated reasoning systems that resolve logical issues, artificial intelligence employs propositional logic.

By adding variables, predicates, and quantifiers, predicate logic expands propositional logic. Predicate logic enables mathematical explanations of attributes shared by groups of items and relationships among entities, as opposed to reasoning simply about entire sentences. For instance, broad assertions like "every customer have an account" or "some patients require additional treatment" can be expressed using predicate logic. Predicate logic is widely used in knowledge representation systems because it offers a flexible mathematical language that can allow intelligent inference and describe complex relationships. The development of symbolic artificial intelligence has been greatly aided by this capacity to express information formally.

Another important area of discrete mathematics is combinatorics, which examines how to count, arrange, and choose objects according to predetermined rules. Even while counting seems straightforward in daily life, there are a huge number of possible combinations in many computer issues. In scheduling, route planning, feature selection, resource allocation, gaming, and optimization, artificial intelligence faces combinatorial problems. Combinatorics-based mathematical methods enable intelligent systems to efficiently assess various options without examining each one individually. When solving issues with millions or billions of potential solutions, this efficiency becomes even more crucial.

Another potent idea in computer science and discrete mathematics is recursion. By repeatedly applying the same process to progressively smaller versions of the original problem, recursive approaches solve difficult problems. Because large structures frequently consist of smaller structures with similar qualities, many algorithms naturally follow recursive patterns. Recursive thinking is useful for tree traversal, divide-and-conquer algorithms, dynamic programming, and symbolic reasoning. Recursion is often used in artificial intelligence to solve optimization problems, analyze hierarchical data, and explore search spaces.

By offering mathematical models for representing relationships among objects, graph theory extends discrete mathematics. A graph is made up of vertices, also known as nodes, that are joined by edges that show links or interactions. Graph theory focuses on abstract networks that represent relationships among entities, in contrast to graphical charts that show numerical functions. Graphs can be used to depict biological routes, financial transactions, social media platforms, transportation systems, communication networks, and recommendation systems. Because of its adaptability, graph theory has become one of the most crucial mathematical tools in network research and artificial intelligence.

Vertices represent the individual entities in a graph. Vertices can represent individuals, places, websites, documents, proteins, sensors, computers, or logical concepts, depending on the application. The connections between these entities—such as friendships, linkages, communication channels, roadways, trades, or biological interactions—are referred to as edges. Artificial intelligence can identify structural linkages that might otherwise go unnoticed by representing data as connected graphs rather than discrete records. These connections frequently hold important data for forecasting, categorization, and decision-making.

Depending on the characteristics of their edges, graphs can be divided into several categories. Mutual relationships with no clear direction, such as friendships or partnerships, are represented by undirected graphs. One-way relationships, such as hyperlinks between web pages or follower relationships on social media, are represented as directed graphs, which assign directions to edges. Numerical values that represent trip times, distances, probabilities, or relationship strengths are associated with edges in weighted graphs. To ensure that mathematical representations accurately reflect real-world events, artificial intelligence selects alternative graph models based on the features of the problem being tackled.

Two key concepts in graph theory are paths and connectedness. A path is made up of a series of connected vertices that lead via successive edges from one place to another. The ability of two vertices to connect via accessible pathways is referred to as connectivity. While communication networks assess connectivity to ensure reliable information sharing, navigation systems employ graph algorithms to find efficient routes. Similarly, artificial intelligence relies on graph structures to solve routing problems, plan actions, analyze social networks, and understand relationships across vast amounts of data.

Trees are a unique class of graphs with a hierarchical structure devoid of cycles. Trees are especially effective in representing hierarchical information because each pair of vertices in a tree is connected by exactly one path. Tree architectures are inherent in file systems, organizational charts, family dynamics, and decision-making procedures. Decision trees are a popular machine learning technique that classify observations by repeatedly splitting the dataset based on informative features. Until the system makes a final prediction, each branching decision reduces the range of possibilities. Decision trees are useful tools in artificial intelligence because of their efficiency and interpretability.

Algorithms for graph traversal offer methodical ways to investigate network structures. While depth-first search investigates entire routes before going back to earlier branching, breadth-first search looks at nearby vertices level by level. Numerous computational tasks, including connection analysis, cycle detection, shortest-path discovery, and state-space exploration, are supported by these techniques. Graph traversal is used by artificial intelligence in robotics, knowledge graph analysis, automated planning, game-playing algorithms, and recommendation systems. Large networks can be processed by intelligent systems with minimal computational resources thanks to effective graph structure discovery.

One of the most useful uses of graph theory is in shortest-path algorithms. Finding the most effective path through interconnected networks is necessary for many real-world systems. Autonomous robots use shortest-path computations to navigate unfamiliar settings, transportation services determine optimal driving routes, and communication systems reduce transmission delays. Artificial intelligence can quickly calculate effective routes, even in networks with millions of connections, thanks to algorithms such as Dijkstra's and related optimization techniques.

Another significant optimization challenge in discrete mathematics is introduced by graph coloring. The goal is to minimize the overall number of colors used while allocating colors to vertices so that neighboring vertices receive distinct colors. Graph coloring simulates real-world scheduling, frequency assignment, test scheduling, processor allocation, and resource management issues despite its abstract look. Graph coloring techniques are used by artificial intelligence to maximize efficiency, avoid disputes, and coordinate conflicting operations.

One of the most significant uses of graph theory in artificial intelligence nowadays is in knowledge graphs. Knowledge graphs represent data as interconnected networks of entities and interactions rather than as discrete facts. Knowledge graphs are used by search engines, digital assistants, recommendation engines, and semantic web technologies to comprehend context, provide complex answers, and identify indirect connections between concepts. Compared to conventional databases, intelligent systems are better able to reason about information thanks to their structured representation.

Graph neural networks, which integrate deep learning methods with graph theory, are a recent development in artificial intelligence. Conventional neural networks are good at processing structured numerical arrays, but they often struggle with irregular network architectures. By enabling information to flow between connected vertices while preserving graph structure, graph neural networks circumvent this restriction. In the fields of molecular biology, fraud detection, recommendation systems, transportation optimization, and social network analysis, these models have shown impressive results. Their evolution demonstrates how cutting-edge artificial intelligence research is still motivated by classical graph theory.

Additionally, discrete mathematics plays a major role in cybersecurity. By using communication channels to connect devices, computer networks organically create graphs. Security experts examine these graph structures to identify weaknesses, trace cyberattacks, spot unusual communication patterns, and bolster network defenses. By fusing machine learning and graph analysis, artificial intelligence enhances these capabilities and enables more precise identification of abnormalities and new security risks.

Analytical reasoning, logical thinking, abstraction, and methodical problem-solving are all strengthened by studying discrete mathematics and graph theory. Students gain the ability to establish rigorous arguments, identify structural linkages, represent complicated systems mathematically, and create effective algorithms that can solve difficult computational problems. Beyond artificial intelligence, these abilities are used in engineering, finance, biology, telecommunications, logistics, and many other scientific fields where computational thinking and network analysis are increasingly crucial.

To sum up, graph theory and discrete mathematics offer essential mathematical underpinnings for contemporary computing and artificial intelligence. These fields enable intelligent systems to efficiently organize knowledge, describe relationships, analyze complex structures, and solve computational problems using sets, logic, combinatorics, recursion, graphs, trees, and network analysis. In particular, graph theory provides sophisticated mathematical models for depicting the interrelated data that underpins social media, biological research, recommendation engines, communication networks, transportation systems, and knowledge representation. Discrete mathematics and graph theory will continue to be crucial for creating intelligent systems that can reason effectively, find meaningful relationships, and solve complex real-world problems accurately, efficiently, and reliably as artificial intelligence develops toward more interconnected and data-rich environments.

Information Theory and Mathematical Modeling

Artificial intelligence, computer science, communication systems, data science, and other engineering specialties all heavily rely on information theory and mathematical modeling, two closely related areas of mathematics. Effective information gathering, representation, transmission, and interpretation are essential to artificial intelligence, and these processes require mathematical concepts that clarify how data can be quantified, organized, and converted into useful knowledge. While mathematical modeling gives ways to describe real-world systems using equations, algorithms, and structured mathematical relationships, information theory offers a quantitative foundation for comprehending data, uncertainty, and communication. When combined, these fields allow intelligent systems to evaluate enormous volumes of data, identify significant patterns, make the best choices, and resolve challenging issues in a variety of real-world applications.

One of the most important resources in modern society is information. Information that can be gathered and examined is represented by every digital image, written document, financial transaction, medical record, scientific observation, and online contact. However, unless information can be accurately expressed, efficiently communicated, securely stored, and appropriately processed, it has little value. By offering mathematical techniques for quantifying information and understanding how uncertainty affects communication, information theory addresses these issues. Communication networks, data compression techniques, machine learning systems, and intelligent technologies that rely on precise data processing are all designed using these ideas.

The notion that information lowers uncertainty is one of the main tenets of information theory. There could be several outcomes, each with varying likelihood, before learning new knowledge. Uncertainty decreases as new information becomes available because some options are eliminated and others become more likely—similar to this, artificial intelligence works by continuously lowering uncertainty as it examines more facts. While an image recognition algorithm enhances its prediction after analyzing visual data, a medical diagnosis system gains confidence after evaluating laboratory results. The mathematical vocabulary for characterizing these decreases in uncertainty comes from information theory.

One of the most crucial metrics in information theory is entropy. Entropy measures how uncertain or unpredictable a source of information is. Because future results can be predicted with a high degree of confidence, a highly predictable process has low entropy. On the other hand, because many different outcomes remain equally plausible, a highly unpredictable process has high entropy. Entropy is used in artificial intelligence to assess decision-making procedures, quantify forecast uncertainty, and calculate the amount of information gleaned from fresh observations. As a result, entropy serves as a statistical measure of how useful data is for learning and forecasting.

The idea of entropy is directly expanded upon by information gain. Information gain quantifies the degree to which uncertainty is diminished following the observation of fresh facts or a specific choice. When choosing features for classification, decision tree algorithms—which are frequently employed in machine learning—strongly rely on information acquisition. The algorithm selects the attribute that reduces uncertainty the most at each stage, resulting in more precise and effective predictions. By reducing unnecessary computations, this mathematical technique enables intelligent systems to identify the most informative features in large datasets.

Another useful application of information theory is data compression. Digital files frequently contain redundant information that could be expressed more effectively without altering their main content. By removing redundancy while preserving crucial information, compression algorithms reduce storage requirements and transmission times. Large datasets that include text, photos, videos, and sensor measurements are often processed using artificial intelligence. These systems can store and analyze massive amounts of data while reducing computational costs and communication delays through effective compression algorithms.

Information theory also plays a major role in communication systems. Errors may arise from interference, noise, or hardware constraints when data is transferred over computer networks, wireless signals, satellite links, or optical fibers. To maintain the accuracy of transmitted communications, information theory offers mathematical techniques for identifying and correcting these errors. Even when some of the transmitted data is corrupted, error-correcting codes enable communication systems to restore the original data. Because they frequently rely on continuous data flow across various systems, artificial intelligence applications such as Internet of Things devices, driverless cars, and remote medical monitoring benefit from these dependable communication techniques.

Artificial intelligence and information theory are closely related to probability theory. The possibility of certain events determines the substance of the information. Because they lessen ambiguity more than highly predictable events, rare or unexpected events typically transmit more information. Predictions, classifications, and recommendations are guided by machine learning algorithms that assess probabilities for various outcomes. Mathematical techniques for analyzing these probabilities and assessing the effectiveness of learning algorithms are provided by information theory.

Information theory is enhanced by mathematical modeling, which provides structured representations of real-world systems. An abstract depiction of a system using mathematical equations, functions, variables, and relationships is called a mathematical model. Models focus on the key elements that influence system behavior rather than trying to replicate every aspect of reality. Mathematical models are crucial to artificial intelligence because they simplify difficult real-world issues so that computers can examine and resolve them methodically.

Finding the essential variables that characterize a system is the first step in the modeling process. Physical measurements, financial indicators, biological traits, consumer preferences, environmental factors, and a host of other numbers can all be considered variables. Mathematical relationships are created to explain how changes in one variable affect others when pertinent variables have been chosen. Depending on the problem, equations, probability distributions, graphs, matrices, or computational methods may be used to depict these relationships. These mathematical structures are used by artificial intelligence programs to identify trends, forecast outcomes, and maximize choices.

One of the key features of mathematical modeling is simplification. Systems in the real world frequently exhibit considerable complexity and numerous interrelated components. Analyzing every detail would be unfeasible or impractical. Therefore, by focusing on the most important variables and omitting less important features, mathematical models simplify reality. Artificial intelligence systems can generate valuable predictions without requiring infinite computational resources, thanks to this compromise between simplicity and accuracy. While maintaining computing efficiency and mathematical manageability, effective models capture crucial behavior.

There are various uses for mathematical models. Deterministic models are appropriate for systems governed by predictable physical laws because they assume that similar inputs always yield identical outputs. By assigning probabilities to various outcomes, probabilistic models account for uncertainty and reflect the variability frequently seen in real-world scenarios. Because human behavior, financial markets, weather patterns, and biological processes all entail uncertainty that cannot be disregarded, artificial intelligence often relies on probabilistic models. The features of the system under study and the goals of the analysis determine which model is best.

A potent type of mathematical modeling is machine learning. Algorithms examine historical data during training to learn mathematical functions that explain correlations between variables. Predictions for data that has never been seen before can then be produced by these learned models. Different mathematical approaches to modeling complex interactions include Bayesian models, neural networks, support vector machines, decision trees, and linear regression. Each model aims to identify patterns that enable intelligent systems to make precise predictions while adjusting to new knowledge, despite the differences in their mathematical frameworks.

In mathematical modeling, optimization is crucial. To increase performance, a model's parameters frequently need to be changed after it has been built. Optimization methods find parameter values that optimize desired goals or minimize prediction mistakes. One of the most popular optimization methods in AI is gradient descent, which iteratively updates model parameters using the gradient of the loss function until acceptable results are obtained. Mathematical models would not be useful tools for learning from data without optimization; instead, they would remain theoretical descriptions.

Another crucial component of mathematical modeling is validation. In addition to explaining past findings, a model should function well in novel contexts. Validation methods assess accuracy, dependability, and generalization by comparing model predictions with independent data. To ensure that learned models capture real underlying patterns rather than just memorizing samples, artificial intelligence researchers split datasets into training and testing subsets. The confidence that mathematical models will remain useful in real-world applications is increased by thorough validation.

Many applications of artificial intelligence combine mathematical modeling with information theory. While formally expressing linguistic links, natural language processing models evaluate the probability of word sequences. By converting pixel values into mathematical representations that show objects, forms, and textures, computer vision systems evaluate visual data. Recommendation systems use information-theoretic principles to improve predictive quality while modeling relationships among users, items, and preferences. To safely navigate changing environments, autonomous cars integrate sensor data with mathematical models of motion.

An outstanding illustration of these ideas in action is found in the healthcare industry. Medical artificial intelligence systems use mathematical models trained on massive datasets to assess genetic data, medical pictures, lab results, and patient records. While mathematical models estimate disease probabilities and treatment outcomes, information theory helps identify which medical observations have the greatest diagnostic value. These systems help doctors by offering evidence-based suggestions, recognizing uncertainty, and evolving as new medical data becomes available.

Information theory and mathematical modeling are also heavily used in scientific study. Engineers simulate intricate mechanical structures before construction; biologists use graph-based models to investigate genetic networks; economists create mathematical models to explain financial systems; and climate scientists' model atmospheric processes to forecast future climate change. By analyzing vast databases, uncovering hidden connections, and refining mathematical models using empirical data, artificial intelligence strengthens these initiatives. The combination of mathematical modeling and information theory accelerates scientific research in several fields.

More advanced mathematical models are being created to solve more challenging issues as artificial intelligence develops. Advanced mathematical representations underpinned by information-theoretic concepts are essential to deep learning architectures, generative artificial intelligence, probabilistic graphical models, and reinforcement learning systems. These advancements show that robust mathematical underpinnings capable of effectively representing uncertainty, learning from experience, and analyzing information will remain essential for future advances in artificial intelligence.

To sum up, information theory and mathematical modeling offer essential underpinnings for contemporary computational science and artificial intelligence. Information theory uses mathematical concepts such as entropy and information gain to explain how information can be measured, transmitted, compressed, and evaluated while reducing uncertainty. To facilitate prediction, optimization, simulation, and decision-making, mathematical modeling converts intricate real-world systems into organized mathematical representations. When combined, these fields enable intelligent systems to interact efficiently, comprehend massive datasets, organize knowledge, and continuously adapt to new information. Information theory and mathematical modeling will continue to be crucial for developing intelligent systems that are precise, effective, dependable, and able to handle increasingly complex real-world problems as artificial intelligence spreads into healthcare, finance, engineering, education, environmental science, and innumerable other domains.

Numerical Methods and Computational Efficiency

Modern mathematics, scientific computing, artificial intelligence, engineering, and data science are all supported by the underlying ideas of numerical approaches and computational efficiency. Even though mathematical theory offers equations and formulas that explain real-world phenomena, many real-world issues are too large or complex to be resolved using symbolic mathematics alone. Weather forecasting, financial modeling, scientific simulations, artificial intelligence systems, and engineering design frequently entail millions or even billions of calculations that require effective numerical methods. While computational efficiency ensures that computations are performed precisely, swiftly, and with minimal processing power, numerical approaches provide systematic methods for estimating solutions to mathematical problems. When combined, these domains enable intelligent computers to process enormous volumes of data, solve challenging mathematical problems, and produce practical solutions in a reasonable amount of time.

When perfect answers are either unavailable or computationally prohibitive, numerical methods are mathematical approaches that generate approximations. Simple algebraic formulas are insufficient to solve many mathematical equations found in science and engineering. Rather, computers use iterative algorithms that perform repeated computations to approach increasingly accurate solutions. These approximations often achieve a level of precision sufficient for useful decision-making, even though they may not be entirely accurate. Because machine learning models involve complex optimization problems with millions of adjustable parameters that cannot be solved analytically, artificial intelligence primarily relies on numerical techniques.

A key concept in numerical computation is approximation. Numerical approaches acknowledge that carefully managed approximations often yield highly accurate results while significantly reducing computational effort, rather than demanding complete perfection. For instance, it may require an infinite series to determine the precise values of certain functions. In contrast, numerical algorithms yield highly accurate approximations with a small number of computations. Similar ideas are applied by artificial intelligence, which estimates ideal answers through iterative improvements rather than trying to perform impossible exact calculations. Numerical computational issues because they strike a balance between efficiency and precision.

Numerous numerical algorithms are based on iteration. Iterative approaches start with an initial estimate and continuously improve it until the required degree of accuracy is reached, rather than computing a solution in a single step. By lowering errors according to mathematical laws, each iteration moves the solution closer to the right answer. This same idea underpins machine learning training. Optimization techniques continuously modify model parameters during training, progressively increasing prediction accuracy with each iteration. Large datasets would be impossible for contemporary artificial intelligence systems to learn efficiently without iterative numerical techniques.

One of the earliest instances of numerical approaches is root-finding. Although exact solutions are not always attainable, many mathematical equations require figuring out values that make a function equal to zero. Through methodical computations, numerical techniques like Newton's method and the bisection method estimate these roots. These methods are used in optimization problems, physics, economic modeling, and engineering design. While completing optimization tasks and modifying model parameters during training, artificial intelligence also indirectly engages in root-finding.

Another significant use of numerical techniques is the solution of systems of linear equations. Thousands or millions of simultaneous equations are frequently used in scientific simulations, engineering models, and machine learning techniques. Effective numerical techniques are crucial for such large systems, as direct analytical methods are computationally costly. Decomposition algorithms, iterative solvers, and matrix factorization techniques offer workable solutions that let artificial intelligence systems effectively handle big datasets.

These techniques show how closely numerical analysis and linear algebra are related.

Another useful numerical method for estimating unknown values that fall between known observations is interpolation. Let's say that temperature readings are accessible at particular times of the day. Without additional measurements, interpolation calculates temperatures at intermediate times. Interpolation is used by artificial intelligence in scientific modeling, computer graphics, image processing, and sensor analysis. Interpolation reduces the need for superfluous observations while increasing the continuity and utility of numerical data by intelligently approximating missing values.

Areas under curves and definite integrals without easy analytical solutions can be estimated and evaluated using numerical integration. Motion, energy, probability distributions, and fluid dynamics are just a few of the continuous processes in many physical systems that call for integration. In probabilistic modeling, Bayesian inference, and statistical learning algorithms, where exact mathematical integration is often unattainable, artificial intelligence relies on numerical integration. Approximate numerical techniques retain computational economy while producing sufficiently precise results.

Numerous natural processes, including population expansion, heat transport, chemical reactions, weather patterns, and physical motion, are described by differential equations. However, only a small number of differential equations have accurate solutions. By breaking up continuous processes into numerous small computational steps, numerical methods such as Euler's method and Runge-Kutta techniques approximate solutions. By fusing machine learning and numerical modeling, artificial intelligence enhances computational performance and prediction accuracy in scientific simulations using differential equations.

One of the most significant uses of numerical techniques in artificial intelligence is optimization. The goal of machine learning is to find mathematical models that generalize effectively to new data while minimizing prediction errors. Through repeated numerical computations, optimization techniques modify millions or even billions of model parameters. By pursuing mathematically specified paths that minimize error, gradient descent, stochastic gradient descent, and adaptive optimization techniques progressively enhance model performance. Since precise solutions are typically unattainable for complex neural networks, these optimization processes rely solely on effective numerical computing.

The ability to perform calculations with reasonable precision while using the least time, memory, and processing power is known as computational efficiency. Computational efficiency is becoming increasingly crucial as artificial intelligence systems continue to grow more complex. Scientific simulations, recommendation engines, image recognition systems, and large language models process huge datasets that require trillions of mathematical operations. These systems can reduce energy consumption and hardware requirements while delivering valuable results within realistic time constraints, thanks to efficient algorithms.

Computational complexity analysis is frequently used to assess algorithm efficiency. Complexity metrics describe how computational requirements increase with problem size. When analyzing millions of observations, a technique that works well on small datasets could become unfeasible. To find techniques that can effectively handle ever-larger datasets, artificial intelligence researchers closely examine algorithmic complexity. Whether difficult computational tasks can be accomplished within available computing resources is typically determined by the choice of appropriate algorithms.

Another crucial component of computing performance is memory efficiency. Artificial intelligence systems often analyze large datasets that exceed available computer memory. Large-scale calculations can continue without depleting hardware resources because of effective data structures, compression methods, and memory management techniques. For instance, sparse matrix representations greatly reduce memory consumption in many machine learning applications by storing just relevant numerical values rather than a huge number of zeros.

Increasing computational efficiency now requires parallel computing. Parallel systems split large computing processes into smaller subtasks that are carried out concurrently by several processors, rather than completing calculations sequentially. Because graphics processing units can execute thousands of mathematical operations in parallel, they are especially well-suited for artificial intelligence. For neural network training to effectively handle big datasets, parallel computation is crucial. This hardware acceleration has greatly aided the quick development of deep learning technology.

Another crucial factor in computational mathematics is numerical stability. Because computers represent real numbers with limited precision, rounding errors can accumulate over time. If algorithms are poorly constructed, even small numerical errors can eventually become large computational errors. Stable algorithms that reduce error accumulation while maintaining reliable results are developed by numerical analysts. Numerically stable optimization techniques are beneficial for artificial intelligence because they improve learning accuracy and reduce the likelihood of computational errors during model training.

Applications of artificial intelligence make the value of computational efficiency and numerical techniques abundantly evident. When evaluating digital images, computer vision systems perform billions of matrix operations. Models for natural language processing compute optimization updates, vector transformations, and probabilities over large text sets. Recommendation systems use effective numerical algorithms to process millions of client contacts. While making real-time navigation decisions that require rapid mathematical computation, autonomous cars continuously evaluate sensor data. These advanced AI applications would not be feasible without effective numerical methods.

Computational efficiency is also crucial for scientific study. Climate scientists simulate the vast number of interacting variables in atmospheric systems. Physicists use sophisticated numerical methods to simulate particle interactions. While medical researchers use computational algorithms to study genetic data, engineers use computer simulations to assess structural designs before construction. By speeding up numerical calculations, spotting hidden patterns, and refining mathematical models based on observable data, artificial intelligence is advancing these scientific studies more and more.

The design of algorithms in modern software development places a strong emphasis on computational efficiency. Programmers look for solutions that strike a compromise between scalability, accuracy, memory utilization, execution speed, and maintainability. Developers may concentrate on higher-level problem-solving instead of low-level computational intricacies thanks to numerical libraries, which offer meticulously optimized implementations of popular mathematical operations. Similar to this, highly tuned numerical algorithms that optimize performance across many hardware platforms are incorporated into artificial intelligence frameworks.

Studying numerical techniques fosters useful computational thinking and mathematical reasoning. Approximation, algorithm design, iterative reasoning, error analysis, optimization, and efficiency evaluation are among the skills that learners acquire. These abilities equip students to tackle challenging real-world issues for which precise mathematical answers are either unavailable or impossible. Understanding computational constraints also promotes responsible algorithm design that accounts for both practical implementation and mathematical accuracy.

The significance of numerical techniques and processing efficiency will only grow as artificial intelligence develops. Algorithms that can properly and efficiently conduct massive quantities of calculations are needed for larger datasets, more complicated applications, and more sophisticated models. To increase the capabilities of intelligent systems while reducing computational costs, researchers are continually developing more effective optimization strategies, faster numerical algorithms, specialized computer architectures, and energy-efficient computing approaches.

In conclusion, artificial intelligence, scientific computing, engineering, and contemporary mathematics all rely heavily on numerical techniques and computational efficiency. While computational efficiency guarantees that these computations are carried out swiftly, precisely, and with responsible use of computing resources, numerical approaches offer systematic procedures for approximating solutions to mathematical problems that cannot be solved perfectly. These mathematical concepts enable intelligent systems to process large volumes of data and address complex real-world problems through approximation, iteration, optimization, interpolation, numerical integration, solution of differential equations, and complexity analysis. A strong understanding of numerical techniques and computational efficiency will remain crucial for creating intelligent systems that are dependable, scalable, and capable of handling the expanding computational demands of the future as technology advances and artificial intelligence is increasingly incorporated into science, healthcare, finance, transportation, education, and engineering.

Emerging Mathematical Directions for Future AI Innovations

Innovation in science and technology has always been fueled by mathematics, and with the quick development of artificial intelligence, this influence has only grown. Mathematical concepts that explain patterns, relationships, optimization, probability, and computing have enabled every significant advancement in artificial intelligence, from machine learning and neural networks to computer vision and natural language processing. As artificial intelligence advances, new mathematical concepts are being developed to tackle increasingly difficult problems, including logic, adaptation, efficiency, uncertainty, ethics, and large-scale computation. By enhancing their capacity to learn, make decisions, communicate with people, and address issues once thought beyond the capabilities of computers, these new mathematical paths are shaping the future of intelligent systems. Gaining knowledge of these evolving mathematical frameworks can help one better understand the future of artificial intelligence and how mathematics will continue to spur innovation.

The creation of more sophisticated optimization techniques is one of the most significant new directions.

Because learning algorithms improve by reducing prediction errors while optimizing performance, optimization has always been essential to artificial intelligence. Traditional optimization methods face additional challenges in computational cost, memory usage, and convergence speed as artificial intelligence models grow in size and complexity. Researchers are developing mathematical techniques to navigate highly dimensional optimization problems more effectively. These methods accelerate learning and enhance model stability by combining concepts from calculus, probability, geometry, and numerical analysis. Artificial intelligence systems should be able to learn more quickly, require fewer training examples, and use far less processing power thanks to future optimization techniques.

As artificial intelligence systems process more complex datasets, the significance of high-dimensional mathematics continues to grow. When dealing with hundreds or thousands of dimensions, traditional geometric intuition frequently fails, necessitating the use of new mathematical techniques to comprehend the structure of high-dimensional spaces. To reduce needless complexity and uncover hidden links between variables, researchers are exploring sophisticated geometric approaches. By enhancing dimensionality reduction, feature extraction, and representation learning, these mathematical advancements help artificial intelligence systems find significant patterns more quickly. High-dimensional mathematics will continue to be a crucial field of innovation as data grows in quantity and complexity.

Another interesting area of mathematics that impacts artificial intelligence is topology. Topology is the study of the basic characteristics of spaces and forms that do not change under constant change. Topology looks upon connectedness, continuity, and structural links rather than precise measurements. Topological data analysis in artificial intelligence offers ways to find hidden structures in complicated datasets that conventional statistical methods might miss. These techniques aid researchers in comprehending how biological systems, communication networks, financial markets, and scientific data are organized. Topological techniques are expected to gain more traction as artificial intelligence processes increasingly complex and unstructured data.

One of the most significant mathematical avenues for the future development of artificial intelligence is graph theory. Social media platforms, transportation networks, biological routes, communication infrastructures, and knowledge bases are just a few examples of the many real-world systems that organically form interconnected networks. When graph theory and deep learning are combined to evaluate these intricate interactions, graph neural networks have already shown impressive results. The goal of future mathematics research is to create more effective graph algorithms, enhance graph representations, and enable artificial intelligence to reason over ever-larger and more dynamic networks. Healthcare, cybersecurity, recommendation systems, scientific research, and intelligent communication will all benefit from these developments.

Future artificial intelligence research will continue to rely heavily on probability theory and uncertainty quantification. Intelligent systems must be able to reason under uncertainty because real-world environments involve unpredictable events, shifting circumstances, and incomplete knowledge. By creating richer probability models that capture intricate relationships among variables, emerging mathematical techniques aim to enhance probabilistic reasoning. With increasingly effective inference methods, Bayesian mathematics continues to grow, enabling artificial intelligence systems to update their knowledge as new data becomes available continually. Applications of artificial intelligence in healthcare, autonomous vehicles, finance, and scientific decision-making will be more dependable, transparent, and safe with improved uncertainty estimation.

To address the problems posed by massive amounts of digital data, information theory is also advancing. Artificial intelligence systems must determine which information is useful while disregarding unnecessary or redundant information. To assess knowledge representation, feature relevance, communication efficiency, and learning capability inside intelligent systems, new mathematical techniques expand on classical information theory. Researchers are investigating mathematical metrics that assess the quantity and utility of information. Data compression, communication networks, distributed artificial intelligence, and cooperative learning among several intelligent agents are all anticipated to benefit from these advancements.

Explainable artificial intelligence is another quickly emerging area of mathematics. Although they function as intricate mathematical systems that are challenging for humans to understand, modern deep learning models frequently generate extremely accurate predictions. To quantify decision confidence, identify significant variables, and explain how predictions are generated, researchers are developing mathematical frameworks. These explainability techniques draw from information theory, graph theory, probability, optimization, and linear algebra. Better mathematical explanations will promote responsible applications in public policy, education, law, medicine, and finance while bolstering confidence in artificial intelligence.

As artificial intelligence systems impact judgments that impact people's lives, mathematical modeling of fairness has grown in significance. Researchers are aware that biases may be inadvertently reproduced by mathematical models trained on historical data. The goal of new mathematical techniques is to assess equity across various populations, analyze algorithmic bias, and define fairness. To strike a compromise between forecast accuracy and fairness goals, statistical approaches, optimization strategies, and probability theory are being modified. By ensuring that intelligent systems make judgments that are both efficient and socially responsible, these mathematical advancements support responsible artificial intelligence.

Another fascinating area for artificial intelligence in the future is quantum mathematics. In contrast to traditional computation, quantum computing introduces mathematical concepts based on quantum mechanics. Quantum systems work on quantum states that can represent several possibilities at once, as opposed to just binary values. Researchers are developing new mathematical algorithms for quantum computers, even though practical quantum artificial intelligence is still in its early stages. Eventually, these algorithms might be able to address machine learning, simulation, and optimization issues that are beyond the capabilities of traditional computer systems.

As a mathematical language for explaining interactions among complex systems, category theory has also garnered increasing attention. Category theory, originally developed in abstract mathematics, offers highly general techniques for expressing structures and transformations across a variety of domains. By characterizing learning, thinking, and computing inside a single mathematical framework, these abstract mathematical concepts, according to some academics, may someday unite several fields of artificial intelligence. Category theory shows how abstract mathematics might inspire future computational advancements, even though it remains largely theoretical.

New mathematical research on sequential decision-making is still driven by reinforcement learning. Intelligent agents frequently have to weigh short-term gains against long-term gains when making decisions. To increase learning effectiveness and long-term planning, new mathematical techniques integrate probability, optimization, game theory, and dynamic programming. It is anticipated that future reinforcement learning algorithms would adapt to changing settings more quickly and require fewer training trials. Autonomous robots, intelligent manufacturing systems, individualized education, healthcare planning, and scientific research will all benefit from these mathematical developments.

Another multidisciplinary path linking biology and artificial intelligence is mathematical neuroscience. Despite being modeled after biological brains, artificial neural networks are still merely mathematical approximations of neural activity. Mathematical models of learning, memory, perception, and cognition in biological nerve systems are still being studied by researchers. Neuroscience insights could lead to whole new mathematical frameworks with more adaptable reasoning, ongoing learning, and computation that uses less energy. This interplay between mathematics and biology shows how a better understanding of natural intelligence could benefit future artificial intelligence.

As artificial intelligence models continue to grow in size and complexity, numerical mathematics will continue to be crucial. Large computational resources capable of performing trillions of mathematical operations are needed to train contemporary language models and scientific simulation systems. The goal of emerging numerical algorithms is to increase computational efficiency through improved memory management, parallel processing, adaptive precision, and optimization. In addition to lowering energy consumption, these mathematical advancements enable more complex models to run on current hardware. Effective numerical techniques will be essential to increasing the accessibility of advanced artificial intelligence in scientific research, industry, healthcare, and education.

Future innovation increasingly depends on interdisciplinary mathematical collaboration. Algebra, calculus, geometry, topology, graph theory, probability, statistics, optimization, information theory, and computer mathematics are all now incorporated into artificial intelligence studies. To tackle difficult scientific problems, these mathematical disciplines are becoming increasingly complementary rather than evolving separately. Researchers may create more comprehensive models that can represent various facets of intelligence, learning, reasoning, and communication through this interdisciplinary integration.

Alongside these advances in mathematics, the training of upcoming researchers in artificial intelligence will also change. In addition to traditional mathematical skills, students will need to apply computational thinking to real-world situations while integrating ideas from multiple fields. As new theories continue to expand the capabilities of intelligent systems, solid foundations in mathematical reasoning, abstraction, logical analysis, and modeling will remain crucial. As artificial intelligence advances, mathematical discoveries are expected to emerge continually, making lifelong learning increasingly crucial.

Future AI will also prioritize cooperation between human and intelligent systems. By creating models that enhance transparency, interpretability, dependability, and communication between machines and human users, mathematics will enable this collaboration. Future mathematical frameworks seek to improve decision-making by fusing computing power with human judgment, creativity, and ethical reasoning rather than displacing human knowledge. This cooperative approach reflects the increasing understanding that meaningful human contact is just as important to the development of artificial intelligence as technical competence.

In conclusion, emerging mathematical directions are providing new approaches to learning, reasoning, optimization, uncertainty management, fairness, efficiency, and explainability, influencing the future of artificial intelligence. While tackling increasingly difficult scientific and technological problems, developments in optimization, topology, graph theory, probability, information theory, numerical mathematics, reinforcement learning, quantum mathematics, category theory, and mathematical neuroscience are enhancing the capabilities of intelligent systems. Artificial intelligence can now process larger datasets, operate more effectively, make better decisions, and communicate with people more successfully thanks to these advances in mathematics. Mathematics will continue to be the key language that drives innovation, promotes responsible development, and unlocks the next generation of intelligent technologies capable of solving the world's most difficult problems as artificial intelligence continues to transform healthcare, education, finance, engineering, transportation, environmental science, and countless other fields.

CONCLUSION

Intelligent technologies continue to develop and grow on the solid basis of mathematics. From autonomous systems and deep learning to pattern recognition and predictive modeling, every development in artificial intelligence relies on meticulously crafted mathematical principles that guarantee precision, effectiveness, and dependability. Readers can gain a deeper understanding of both the mechanics of intelligent systems and the thinking that allows machines to learn, adapt, and make wise judgments by delving into these related ideas. This more profound view turns mathematical knowledge from a set of theoretical concepts into a useful instrument for creativity.

Algebra, geometry, calculus, probability, statistics, optimization, and discrete mathematics all work together to promote the creation of contemporary AI applications, as this book's theories have shown. Every subject offers a distinct framework for data analysis, computational problem-solving, and algorithm development that can handle increasingly challenging real-world problems. When combined, these mathematical fields provide a thorough foundation that enables students to approach artificial intelligence with assurance and clarity.

The significance of mathematical literacy will only increase as technology develops. Readers will be able to improve their analytical thinking and adjust to new developments with continued practice, curiosity, and a dedication to lifelong learning. The information acquired from these pages offers a long-lasting framework for investigating cutting-edge technologies, making significant discoveries, and taking part in the continuous evolution of artificial intelligence throughout sectors and society.

Thank you for buying and reading/ listening to our book. If you found this book useful/ helpful please take a few minutes and leave a review on the platform where you purchased our book. Your feedback matters greatly to us.